STAN PACKS

Written by Frances Minters
Illustrated by Sally J. K. Davies

Stan was getting ready for a trip.

4

has so much milk that it does not know how to dispose of it. Is there no end to the greed of the chemical industry? The RSPCA is opposed to the use of this hormone on the grounds that it will place enormous stress on cows being forced to produce much more milk than is natural for them. I agree. I also wonder, if this development should be widely adopted, what additional adverse effects it will have on those who consume such milk. Milk already contains traces of the hormones and antibiotics with which the cows have been treated, and these alone can be the cause of some people's problems.

Cheese

I mention cheese as a separate issue because, apart from it being a cows' milk product, it also contains tyramine, which will affect certain people. Those who are allergic only to the whey of cows' milk may be able to tolerate a hard cheese.

Eggs

Eggs are another common source of allergy, and can produce severe reaction in infants when given for the first time. The yolk and the white should be considered separately although there are those who will not be able to take either. The egg white (or albumen) is the protein and is the more likely culprit. As with milk, when eggs are heated to a high enough temperature, some of the allergenic properties are destroyed, therefore hard-boiled eggs or eggs baked in cakes may be better tolerated by otherwise egg-allergic people.

Pork

Pork is the most acid of all meats and about one in five people are made ill by it. Pigs are fed on very varied diets, which, in turn, may result in adverse reactions. 'Smoked' bacon, unless otherwise stated, is not smoked at all but treated with chemicals.

31

Fish

Fish can be a severe allergen. Even the smell can affect some people. Many fish are scavengers, so this is sometimes the reason why they cause allergy symptoms. There are some exceptions to this, one of which is plaice, and it is therefore relatively safe for the majority of people, which is why I include it in my elimination diet. Watch out for 'smoked' fish. Unless specifically stated as being naturally smoked, it is likely to be coloured with tartrazine if it is yellow, and brown FK if it is brown.

Potatoes
Peas and Beans

These are marginally more likely to cause allergic reactions than other vegetables. Added to this, growth promoters and other chemicals may affect some people. Organically-grown produce, which is becoming more widely available, may be the answer for chemically-sensitive people (the same applies to fruit).

Cereals

Cereals, particularly wheat and corn, are a common cause of allergic illness and, where this applies, less common cereals can be used quite satisfactorily to make up the bulk of a diet. Unfortunately corn is a 'hidden' ingredient in many processed foods, as well as being the most commonly used binder or filler in pills. Not many people know that corn is present in toothpaste and in the gum on envelopes.

Certain people are affected only by the gluten which is to be found in wheat, oats, barley and rye. Gluten-free products can be bought from health food shops or chemists.

Sugar

Sugar is a positive poison to some allergy sufferers. Unfortunately a common manifestation of sugar allergy is aggression or, in more severe reactions, it can cause people to become quite violent. People can be allergic to cane sugar, beet sugar, or both.

Soya
Soya milk is a good alternative to cows' milk and is an excellent source of protein and useful for vegetarians or those with several meat allergies. Unfortunately, it also carries a possible risk for allergy sufferers, and therefore should initially be tested with care.

Yeast
Yeast causes problems for people who are prone to thrush (otherwise known as candida albicans). It is to be found in bread, of course, and in other foods such as cheese, mushrooms, and alcoholic drinks.

Citrus Fruits (Orange, Lemon, Grapefruit and Lime)
Citrus fruits can be a cause of allergic reaction. Where this is the case, avoidance of citric acid (also known as fruit acid) in jams and similar products is necessary. Citric acid is prepared commercially by fermentation.

CHEMICALS

Artificial Colourings
Sensitive people are unable to tolerate many of the artificial colourings (some of which have been banned in other European countries) and other chemical additives in processed foods.

Azo and coal tar dyes are known to cause a wide range of symptoms, of which hyperactivity and learning disabilities in children have been most thoroughly investigated. These colourings can cause sleeplessness, an inability to concentrate, and disruptive behaviour. In adults they can cause depression and many other symptoms.

Tartrazine (E102), a yellow azo dye, was to be found until recently in fruit squashes, most ice-creams, and so-called 'smoked' fish. Due to public pressure, manufacturers have felt obliged to remove this and other azo dyes from some foods and drinks. However, many highly coloured sweets, especially the cheaper brands, still contain them, as do many medicines. Boots the Chemists have recently brought out a whole range of children's medicines which are free from artificial colourings. On the 9 p.m. BBC news on Friday, 13th March 1987, it was reported that the manufacturers estimated that only 0.06% of children suffered adverse effects as a result of consuming tartrazine. As the number was so small, the manufacturers recommended that rather than stopping using it, mothers of sensitive children should simply avoid giving it to them.

This advice is nonsense on several counts. Firstly, there is no miraculous change in adulthood. A tartrazine-sensitive child becomes a tartrazine-sensitive adult. Therefore they should at least say 0.06% of *people*. This amounts to 33,000 individuals — quite a number to go through what can amount to family-breaking traumas. And this is only if their statistics are correct — where do they get them from? They should ask the Hyperactive Children's Support Group if they corroborate their figures. I believe a very different set of statistics would emerge. Tartrazine is only one of several azo dyes which can cause quite devastating effects on those of us who suffer such sensitivities. The manufacturers of artificial additives have a lot to answer for.

A list of 'E' numbers, specifying the azo and coal tar dyes, is given at the back of this book.

Artificial Preservatives

Artificial preservatives can cause adverse reactions, and some are suspected of being carcinogenic (cancer causing). Those of the nitrite/nitrate family are especially implicated (see *E for Additives* by Professor Maurice Hanssen).

Monosodium Glutamate

Monosodium glutamate (or sodium glutamate) is an artificial flavouring used to produce a meaty flavour. It is added to processed soups, sauces, etc. It is also used extensively in Chinese cooking. It can cause adverse reactions, the most common being fainting. I will give you an illustration.

Four of us had been to an allergy conference and were on our homeward journey. We had taken our own lunches but decided to risk eating out since it would be late before we reached home. Meals were chosen with care and a patient waiter answered detailed enquiries.

About two hours later, having dropped off the other two at their homes, I was turning the last corner when a strange voice from the back of the car whispered 'I'm going, I'm going'. Bewildered, I turned round to find Marion slumped across the back seat in a heap, dead to the world. Supressing panic, I drew up at her house, and her husband and I carried her into the bedroom. Looking at her ashen face, like a death mask, it just seemed amazing to me that so many doctors refuse to believe that people can be made ill by what they eat. It took Marion the best part of a week before she recovered. She told me later that there must have been monosodium glutamate in the seafood she had ordered, in spite of the waiter's confident assurance to the contrary.

Other artificial flavourings may also cause problems for sensitive people, so should be treated with caution.

Artificial Stabilisers, Emulsifiers and Anti-oxidants

Artificial stabilisers, emulsifiers and anti-oxidants can also affect many allergic people and are best avoided.

A sensitivity to salicylates, which are processed commercially for use in aspirin and occur naturally in such fruits as apples, oranges, peaches and berries, poses a problem for some allergy sufferers.

I believe everyone would benefit from eating an artificial-additive-free diet, because even if they do not appear to do obvious damage no one knows what the long term effects will be. A food additive may be put through stringent tests to prove its safety, but the interaction of it and an individual body chemistry is another matter entirely.

Some artificial colourings are, at long last, being replaced by natural ones and, unless someone has a specific allergy to one of these, they should do no harm.

The Food Additives Campaign Team (FACT) work very hard to protect our food from additives which are known to produce harmful effects to our health. As they say, 'Additives have never been the subject of a Royal Commission, a public enquiry or recent Parliamentary debate. Decisions are taken without proper consultation with consumers or reference to their elected representatives.' They are pressing for a new national policy and I believe it is in the interests of all of us to give them our support. Further information can be obtained from the Food Additive Campaign Team, c/o The London Food Commission, 88 Old Street, London EC1V 9AR. They have published an *Additives Information Pack*, written by Melanie Miller MSc. It costs £1.50 + 35p p+p, and is obtainable from the Publications Department at the above address.

INHALANT ALLERGENS

Scents, Toiletries

Scents, toiletries, perfumed soaps and all the many other 'smellies' marketed for us to adorn our bodies spell disaster for many allergy sufferers. Unless otherwise stated, these products are made from a range of chemicals. The demand for perfumes is such that it can no longer be met solely from natural ingredients. I have a cutting from *Weekend* magazine (April, 1981) which reads: 'Darling, I just love your benzyl acetate.' That just about sums it up.

Luckily, there are now several perfume-free brands of toiletries available which many people will find satisfactory.

Aerosol Sprays

I feel these must have a special mention. Every time one is used, thousands of droplets remain in the air and are inevitably inhaled. If an aerosol spray is used in a small room or the windows are closed, the greater the concentration inhaled. I see no necessity to use these when just about everything which comes in the form of an aerosol spray can be substituted for something which does not (the only exception I allow myself is the occasional use of an unperfumed hair spray which I use in the garden — to the surprise of passers by!).

Sweden is the first country to ban all aerosol sprays with the exception of medical ones. This action was taken as far back as 1979. Their reason for doing so was because they believe the release of fluorocarbons (which are used as propellants) could affect the earth's ozone layer.

Household Cleaners, Detergents, Washing-up Liquids

The chemicals used in these products often adversely affect allergic people. The reaction may be due to the basic constituents or to the perfumes (some are lemon or pine scented). It is always safer to buy the unscented ones.

Others can be affected by washing-up liquid, so inserting the nozzle of the container into the water before squeezing ensures that no droplets escape into the air. An added precaution is to rinse the dishes so that all traces of the liquid are removed.

Formaldehyde

Formaldehyde, according to my dictionary, is 'a colourless, pungent gas, soluble in water, used in making disinfectants and in the manufacture of plastics'. It is also used in the manufacture of fabrics, air fresheners and in the form of foam in cavity wall insulation. It is something to which many allergic people react — a fact of which they might not always be aware.

Formalin — another reactive substance — is a 40% solution in water of formaldehyde gas used as a disinfectant, deodoriser and preservative.

Gas and Oil

The introduction of North Sea gas has been a major contribution to increased allergic conditions. This is not due to the gas itself, which is odourless, but to the addition of a mercapton to make it smell. Mercaptons are a group of organic compounds which, in certain forms, can be highly toxic by inhalation. Obviously this does not apply to the form in which it is used in North Sea gas. Nevertheless, a fair number of allergic people are sensitive to it. Oil boilers are another potential hazard to allergy sufferers.

Paint and Similar Products

Household paint and other products which give off fumes can cause problems. Gloss paint contains toluene, a coal-tar derivative, which affects many people. Paint manufacturers are aware of this and are working towards non-toxicity. Some gloss paints are water, rather than oil, based. Others advertise a 'low odour finish'. 'Petal' can be mixed with paint to disguise the smell. There is a product known as 'liquid driers' which can be obtained from builders' merchants or trade paint shops — this can be added to the paint to cause the fumes to be dispersed more quickly. This has to be used very sparingly otherwise the paint will crack after drying. Ideally, advice should be sought from someone in the business.

Clinical ecologists, like everyone else, do have their premises painted from time to time. If you are paint-sensitive, it is as well to check before a visit as to whether this has taken place recently.

Petrol Fumes, Tobacco Smoke
An allergy to petrol fumes is quite common. Anyone who suffers this way should avoid going too close to the car in front when travelling by car themselves. When caught in a traffic jam, it is advisable to turn off the heater and close the air vents as they introduce contaminated air from outside. Tobacco smoke can affect some people and is not always easy to avoid. Luckily many restaurants and other public places now have no-smoking areas.

Power Stations and Factory Fumes
Though steps are now being taken to clean up our act, British power stations are largely responsible for the 'acid rain' which is killing forest trees both in Britain and in Scandinavia. 'Acid rain' is caused by the sulphur dioxide emitted from power station chimneys. I too am concerned about forests, rivers and wildlife, but I also think it is time someone worried about the effect this concentrated form of pollution is having on human health. Acid rain has already been implicated in conditions such as Alzheimer's disease, and work in Sweden has associated high background acidity with allergic symptoms.

Factory fumes are another form of unavoidable pollution which could cause less damage if all factories were built well away from areas of habitation.

It is an ironic fact that in my home town we have a pharmaceutical factory on the outskirts which at times belches forth the most evil-smelling grey clouds of concentrated fumes. I know some people who are certainly affected by these, and suspect there are many more who are but do not realise it.

All chemicals are suspect, and if inhaled in sufficient concentration would be toxic to anyone. For chemically-sensitive people life has become almost impossible, and some are virtually housebound.

It is as well to be aware of potential hazards before introducing any new chemical into your home. Chemicals are hidden everywhere. Furniture made of chipboard, for instance, contains formaldehyde. Many artificial-fibre carpets can exude noxious fumes, though these do subside over time. These are just two examples. There are many others.

A very good piece of advice for all chemically-sensitive people was given to me by a clinical ecologist. 'If you can smell it,' he said, 'suspect it.'

NATURAL ALLERGENS

Grass, Flower and Tree Pollens, Pine Trees
The months of June and July are no joke for anyone allergic to grass pollen — and many people are. Hay fever, asthma, rhinitis and allied symptoms can be very distressing. People who have this problem are at a disadvantage when sitting examinations which, for reasons best known to the examiners, usually take place at this time of year. Straw and hay can affect people too. Flower pollens are another source of allergen, as are tree pollens. I met a

man who went through the whole process of an elimination diet only to discover that he was allergic to the pine trees which surrounded his garden. He moved and became well again.

Indoor plants must not be forgotten, particularly those with hairy leaves such as primula. These can cause swelling of the eyes and other symptoms such as skin rashes.

House Dust Mites and Bed Mites

We all have these in our homes. There is no getting away from them, so it is very bad luck on those to whom they cause an allergic reaction. This is more of a problem for women who usually do the housework.

For people who are allergic to house dust, hoovering is preferable to brushing — dusting with a damp cloth is better than a dry one. A mask can be worn which may help, otherwise desensitising is the only answer (or better still, avoid housework altogether!).

Feathers

There are not too many of these around now that we live in a polyester era, but down-filled duvets may not suit everyone. Look out for old cushions, which may still be feather filled.

Animal Dander

It is a sad fact that people are occasionally allergic to their own animals. Before you look for another home for your pet, do be *sure* it *is* the cause, because there are so many other possibilities. Also, if rehousing the pet is going to cause the allergy-sufferer much distress (not to mention the animal) it is definitely worth discussing your particular circumstances with your doctor to see if a medication might be used instead.

Mould and Damp

Many allergic people suffer adverse reactions as a result of coming into contact with mould or damp. Apart from the obvious situations where this exists, mould growths can gather in air conditioners (which is why some people become unwell in offices but are symptom-free in their own homes). Dampness and cold rooms in houses can lead to asthma and bronchitis and breathing problems generally. It may help if a member of the family who suffers this way can change to a south or west facing bedroom.

Climate
The ability to tolerate climatic changes differs from one individual to another. The rare air of mountains will be beneficial to all allergy sufferers, especially those with breathing problems, but also those with chemical sensitivities.

Some people have to avoid damp or cold climates, especially those with asthmatic/bronchial/arthritic problems. Others will be affected by cold north-east winds. The majority of sufferers will be better in warm, sunny climes. A few are positively sun-sensitive, though reactions vary. Some people who have a dry eczematous skin may find it clears up completely in warm sunshine. However, prolonged over-exposure to sun can cause skin cancer.

OCCUPATIONAL AND LIFESTYLE RISKS

Industrial Disease (Pneumoconiosis)
Industrial diseases are, of course, diseases in their own right and not allergies. I feel I must give them a mention, however, as over the years one or two people have contacted me who, on close questioning, have seemed likely to be suffering from an industrial disease. Unlike the

allergy sufferer, there are sadly no suggestions I can offer for such symptoms, and with much regret I have felt obliged to tell them so.

The better known industrial diseases are silicosis (caused by the inhalation of fine sand or granite particles), anthracosis (caused by the inhalation of coal dust), and asbestosis (caused by the inhalation of asbestos dust).

Medicines

Nearly all medicines contain artificial colourings, sometimes several, and possibly other artificial additives as well. I have always found chemists who were willing to make up an antibiotic without colouring if it was at all possible, and in general chemists are very helpful.

Many drugs can cause side effects. As doctors seldom mention this — with the possible exception of penicillin-related drugs — people should take it into consideration themselves, and report back to their doctors any new symptoms which have appeared since they started taking the new drug.

It has been estimated that there are now about three million tranquilliser addicts in Britain, more than all the users of 'hard' drugs put together. The group of drugs known as the benzodiazepines (which includes many commonly prescribed tranquillisers) has a dependency potential much higher than was anticipated. It can take more than a year for patients to be free from the distressing withdrawal symptoms imposed by these drugs. Anyone wishing to come off tranquillisers (or any other drug) must do so under the guidance of their doctor. Expert advice can be found in a book called *Coming Off Tranquillisers*, by S.A. Trickett (see the reading list at the back of this book).

The Pill

Oral contraceptives are steroids. As such they can cause serious hormonal side-effects. Dr Ellen Grant, who was a clinical assistant at migraine clinics between 1972 and 1979, has done in-depth studies on the pill, and is most concerned about the common practice of prescribing pill hormones to teenagers for period problems or contraception. Younger women are especially likely to develop serious chemical imbalances leading to multiple allergies and long-term reproductive difficulties.

Smoking

People who smoke have been found to have raised blood carbon monoxide levels. Again, in her studies of migraine, Dr Grant has found the incidence of migraine and other allergies is higher in long-term smokers than short-term or non-smokers.

Some people become allergic or reactive to tobacco smoke itself. This is more likely to happen to susceptible children or adults who live with a smoker in the family. Dr Grant tells me that it is now known that smokers are likely to be zinc-deficient and have zinc-deficient children who, in turn, may be very sensitive to, and highly aware of, the fumes of tobacco smoke.

Dr Grant is now a consulting specialist in allergy, migraine, dyslexia and preconception care, and I am grateful to her for her advice on the above subjects.

Alcohol

Alcohol carries many hazards. It is necessary to consider the content of each alcoholic drink individually. Most contain several ingredients.

Wines and sherries are commonly made from grapes. Red wine contains an amino-acid called tyramine (as do chocolate and cheese) which disagrees with quite a large number of people, some of whom will be able to take white wine which is tyramine-free.

Many of the cheaper imported wines contain a preservative which may be only one of twenty permitted additives. The ground in which the grapes have been grown may have been treated with chemicals which is another potential risk. However, a wide range of organic wines is now available.

Beer is made from hops, but it contains other ingredients including yeast. It is worth knowing that the constituents of beer can vary.

Gin is made from juniper; whiskey from wheat, barley or rye; rum from cane sugar.

To sum up — all alcoholic drinks contain yeast, most contain sugar, and some contain artificial additives. There are those who may be allergic to alcohol *per se*, in which case they will need to give it up altogether.

People who suffer from the effects of alcohol fit into one of three categories. Either they drink too much, or they are allergic to it, or they fall somewhere between the two.

I have two articles kindly provided by *The Daily Telegraph*. One is headed '14 million working days lost through hangovers' (October 15th, 1986) and the other 'Heavy drinkers prone to brain damage by 35'. The latter describes a study published in the *Lancet* which was carried out by a team of doctors in Denmark.

There are organisations and counsellors who work with alcoholics, though not many people yet seem to be aware of just how important allergy is in relation to alcohol. Sometimes the minutest amount of alcohol can cause the most amazing effects.

I once knew a woman called Pat, about forty years old, very smart and highly respectable. Several of us had been to a meeting which finished early, so we decided we would go to our olde worlde village pub. I sat next to Pat and was interested to see that she drank a non-alcoholic drink. I asked her if there was any particular reason and she told me this story.

Her husband had taken her and their daughter to a restaurant in London. She always avoided alcohol at all costs, so drank only lemonade. A lovely meal was had by all, finishing up with, in Pat's case, a gorgeous-looking creamy trifle. On the way back to the car they passed a night club advertising voluptuous girls doing the dance of the seven veils. An extraordinary thing happened. Highly respectable Pat decided that anything they could do she could do better and to the acute embarrassment of her husband and daughter she announced that she was about to do a striptease. She had to be hustled, protesting loudly, back to the car. The next day, of course, she was horrified to learn what she had almost done. No prizes for guessing. It was a *sherry* trifle.

Bright and Flickering Lights

For some migraine or epilepsy sufferers, coming into contact with bright or flickering lights, even television, can be enough to trigger an attack.

Irradiation

There are reports that we may before long have our food subjected to nuclear radiation to prolong its freshness. The government's Advisory Committee on Irradiated Foods has said that there is 'no danger' to public health from this treatment.

I asked a clinical ecologist friend for his views on the subject. He replied, 'Vitiation of foodstuffs has been the worst form of pollution so far. It looks as though that form of pollution is to be increased'. I understand that the process 'bombards food with cobalt-60 gamma rays'. I have no idea exactly what that means, but I do know that I don't like the sound of it one little bit.

The London Food Commission is against the over-hasty legislation of food irradiation and have started a food irradiation campaign calling for the current ban on irradiation to remain in place until it is proven safe, wholesome, good for the food, and needed.

Irradiation has attracted enormous interest and opposition both from individuals and from concerned organisations. The London Food Commission commissioned a Marplan Opinion Poll which showed overwhelming support for maintaining the current ban on food irradiation — 84% said it should remain. Further information can be obtained from the Director, Dr Tim Lang, The London Food Commission, 88, Old Street, London ECIV 9AR, or from the book *Food Irradiation — The Facts* by Tony Webb and Tim Lang, published by Thorsons.

AIDS
It has been suggested by a group of scientists that AIDS may be rampant in our society because the active ingredient in a pesticide can break down the immune system leaving people more vulnerable to the AIDS virus and other diseases (*The Sunday Telegraph*, Nov 16th, 1986). Whilst allergy sufferers have an over-active immunological response, AIDS sufferers have an under-active one. Have we really had to wait for the AIDS virus for scientists to realise that a chemical can damage the immune system? What about all the other chemicals which they allow so freely into our society? Perhaps now that work is going to be done on the failings of the immune system, the long-suffering allergics might also get some help.

Lead
The effects of lead are one of our main environmental hazards. Here are a few tips to prevent a build-up of lead poisoning:

— Try to avoid inhaling the exhaust fumes of cars. Be especially careful with children in pushchairs who are at car exhaust level.

— Beware of old and peeling paint which may be a source of lead.

— Run water from the cold tap first thing in the morning to clear the pipes.

47

- Wash all fruit and vegetables thoroughly, stripping off the outer leaves of green vegetables.

- Get your family to wash their hands before eating.

- If you wish to eat or drink from hand-made pottery, check first that the glaze is lead-free.

Aluminium

In recent years aluminium pans have been the subject of much investigation. Researchers have found that when fluoride is present in cooking water, a chemical reaction appears to cause a dramatic increase in the amount of aluminium released into the cooking water, especially when cooking acid foods like tomatoes or cabbage. Judging from the scrubbed appearance of my aluminium pan whenever I cook rhubarb, I am sure this is one such food.

Aluminium pans are best replaced by Pyrex and enamel. Avoid using aluminium foil and canned foods whenever possible. The aluminium compound, alum, is used as a cleaning agent in many water supplies, and undoubtedly some alum passes into our drinking water.

Researchers have also found an association between aluminium and Alzheimer's disease. Some foods naturally absorb aluminium from the soil. Tea is a prime example of this.

DISCOVERING YOUR ALLERGENS

Discovering Your Allergens

There are three things which should be taken into consideration when people feel their symptoms are allergy-induced. In the short term these are food and inhalant allergens and, in the long term, the immune system, which must be built up to raise the allergy tolerance level, thereby regaining a good standard of health (see the section on the immune system, page 60). Where allergy is concerned, neither age nor the period of suffering is any bar to recovery.

Not everyone needs to face the rigours of an elimination diet. If you are only ill at certain times of the year, this points to the possibility of some seasonal environmental allergy for which, if it is unavoidable, you may require temporary medication from your doctor.

If you are symptom-free when away from home, even though you are eating approximately the same diet, this points to something in your home environment causing your symptoms. Similarly, if you only have the symptoms while at work, you must work out the differences relating to the environment and what you eat and drink there (I know two cases of men who turned out to be allergic to the machine-produced additive-contaminated coffee they consumed at work but could tolerate the purer brand they drank at home).

Anyone who has severe but intermittent symptoms, such as a migraine, should be able to identify their allergen or allergens by making a list of where they were, what they did and what they ate and drank during the twenty four hours prior to starting their symptoms. By doing this two or three times, a common denominator should emerge.

People who have 'good' days and 'bad' days can, if they choose, use the diet of a 'good' day as a basic elimination diet instead of the recommended one, providing they felt quite well upon waking the morning after a 'good' day. Only if this system fails will an elimination diet then become necessary.

Elimination Diet

Having established that your doctor does not wish to give you any tests which are unrelated to allergy, you are now ready to embark on an elimination diet. Choose a period when your commitments are minimal, because you will need time to concentrate on getting well. For a woman, the best time is just after she has finished menstruating.

If you suffer from severe reactions you can gradually wean yourself on to this diet if you wish, thereby cutting down on the severity of any possible withdrawal symptoms. I believe that people who suffer from acute depression, severe asthma or epilepsy should only do this under medical supervision.

Possible inhalant allergens in the home environment should wherever possible be removed whilst undertaking the diet, so as to avoid confusion. Ideally, anyone working should do this over a holiday period because there may be unavoidable inhalant allergens in their place of work.

The principle of this diet is to eat only those things to which people are *less* likely to be allergic. This takes a great deal of will-power, and the support of family and friends is of enormous help.

The diet must be taken for *at least* five days, but preferably a week. In some rare cases up to two weeks may be required to give the system time to eliminate any offending foods. During this time, withdrawal symptoms may be experienced.

On average people find that they feel increasingly unwell for the first few days of the diet, but nearer the end of the week they will begin to feel very much better. New foods should not be introduced until this happens.

Two teaspoonsful of Epsom salts in half a pint of water taken at the beginning to clear the system will lessen the withdrawal symptoms, but you are advised not to leave your home until after these have taken effect!

You are recommended to eat or drink something every 2–3 hours, and to take plenty of *those foods which are allowed*. It is advisable to keep a record of *all* foods and drinks taken and any reactions experienced.

Toothpaste should not be used (sodium bicarbonate is a good substitute), otherwise corn allergies will not withdraw.

Even the finest trace of food (such as licking a finger whilst cooking) may prevent withdrawal.

Anyone who feels they cannot face this diet, or anyone who feels that such an austere diet is not necessary in their particular circumstances, can use the elimination diet outlined in the children's section (page 86). Also, if anyone feels sure that one of the following foods disagrees with them, another fresh food of the same category can be substituted.

My suggested elimination diet is:

Fresh lamb

Fresh plaice

Fresh pears ⎫ If these are to be stewed, remem-
Fresh cabbage ⎭ ber to use bottled water.

Bottled water   This must be in a glass bottle, e.g. Perrier Water, Malvern Water.

Sea salt

Not everyone suffers withdrawal symptoms, but many people do. It depends on what you are allergic to, how quickly you get a reaction, and how often you take a given food or drink. Each person may suffer different types of reactions with different foods, and varying delays before the reaction appears.

The average response is to start withdrawal symptoms on the first or second day, feel worse on the third, and by the fourth or fifth start feeling much better. Don't be disappointed if this takes a little longer.

Reintroducing Foods

So now you are feeling much better! This is the time to start reintroducing new foods. Prior to this you should test your tap water and, if it causes a reaction, you will have to continue using bottled water for the time being.

You want to start with the foods least likely to cause problems. These are fruits (with the exception of citrus fruits), vegetables (with the exception of potatoes, peas and beans) and meat (with the exception of pork). Introduce these singly and in their natural form, take small quantities to start with, and take only one in each twenty-four hour period because of the possibility of a delayed reaction.

If you remain well over a twenty-four hour period, then that food can be added to your 'safe' diet. If not it must be eliminated, and you should not start another food until you are feeling better. Keep a list as you go along.

Some doctors recommend that unpleasant reactions can be relieved by taking two teaspoonsful of sodium bicarbonate and one teaspoonful of potassium bicarbonate in a glass of warm water. My personal experience was that this made me so violently sick that the symptoms seemed preferable. For this reason I would suggest cutting down the dose to half or less on the first occasion. Potassium bicarbonate is sometimes hard to come by, but the sodium bicarbonate on its own will give some relief.

A walk in the fresh air, particularly if you happen to live by the sea, will be found to be beneficial as it will supply extra oxygen to the blood stream.

If, after following this regime, you feel you are left with too few foods to constitute a balanced diet (in spite of supplementing it with the necessary vitamins and minerals) you have three choices.

— You can consult a medically qualified clinical ecologist who practises desensitising treatment. This is, so far, not readily available on the NHS (though some National Insurance schemes now cover such treatment) and, because of the limited number of doctors working in this field and the large number of people seeking treatment, there may be a delay in obtaining appointments. Also many doctors charge high fees. All prefer, and some require, a referral from your GP.

— You can seek the advice of a dietition so that he or she can balance your diet with alternative, less well-known foods.

— You can try the more unusual foods yourself to replace the ones you have eaten in the past. Because sensitivity usually occurs as a result of a build-up of regular exposure to an allergen over a period of time, you are less likely to be affected by these new foods. The chances are you will not develop a sensitivity to them if you rotate them on a four-day basis.

Regaining A Tolerance to Foods

If you have been able to make use of the information you have read so far, you will know that the well-known phrase 'you are what you eat' (or drink or smell) applies to you. The extent of your recovery depends upon the degree to which you are affected, your own circumstances, your will-power, and maybe a bit of good luck thrown in.

After discovering and eliminating your worst allergens, and when you have remained well for some time, you will find that some previous, lesser allergens can now be tolerated because you have raised your allergy threshold.

It is advisable to rotate your foods from now on so that you avoid eating the same foods every day. Doctors often advise a four-day rotation diet (eating different foods each day for four days and then starting again). This precaution is worth following as far as possible because it minimises the chances of developing new allergies. Some people may not have enough different suitable foods to make this a practical proposition, and will just have to do the best they can.

Fixed Allergies

Tolerance to your fixed allergies, which should only constitute 20% of your problems, will never be regained. These foods should be avoided for the rest of your life. They are likely to be the ones which have caused you the most severe reactions.

Cyclic Allergies

Your cyclic allergies, constituting the remaining 80%, can probably be tolerated at some stage of your life providing you only take them from time to time. Tolerance varies in each individual and you will have to discover by trial and error just how often you can take each one without ill effect. Over the years, one's cyclic allergies do tend to change, both in the things to which one is allergic and the symptoms they produce.

Masked Allergies

Both fixed allergies and cyclic allergies can be masked allergies, which means that you temporarily feel better after eating or drinking certain foods (as with alcohol for the alcoholic). This boost may last for several hours before you relapse into your chronically unwell condition. You may return to the offending food again, not realising that this is a subconscious action in order to feel better, thereby setting the cycle in motion again. If you find you are craving a food or a drink, you are likely to be allergic to it. Coffee is a prime example of this.

Different Forms of Allergy Testing
Rule number one in allergy testing is: beware of anyone who claims to 'cure' allergies. There is no cure. There is avoidance or desensitisation, but not a cure.

I believe that in the majority of cases an elimination diet together with an avoidance of inhalant allergens — as far as this is practicable — will produce the most conclusive results.

Unfortunately, not everyone seems willing or able to follow this regime, and some people are really too ill to do so. In these circumstances they are best referred to a clinical ecologist, most of whom have alternative methods of discovering allergens. Very severely allergic people should certainly be in the hands of clinical ecologists: However, these doctors are nearly all in private practice and their treatment will require several, maybe many, visits. Personal phone calls from patients to doctors may also be charged for. Their fees can be expensive. I have known people who have spent a great deal of money in the pursuit of allergy treatment.

My comments on the following forms of testing are based on two criteria — whether in my contact with thousands of people over a ten year period they have reported benefiting from them, and whether I can see any scientific reason why they should work.

Enzyme Potentiated Desensitizisation
EPD was first developed by Dr Len McEwen in 1966. When I was very ill and no one knew how to treat me,

I read of Dr McEwen's vaccine treatment in Dr Richard Mackarness' book *Not All in the Mind*, and asked to be referred to him. During the inevitable long waits beforehand in his surgery, I made a point of questioning other patients and was surprised to find universal praise of the success of his vaccine. Most people I spoke to were hay fever or asthma patients, but a few were multiple food allergy sufferers like myself. I even spoke to a man who told me he suffered from schizophrenia, but with regular EPD treatment this was kept at bay.

For myself I found this form of treatment involved an adverse reaction for anything from a week to ten days followed by several weeks of feeling much better. Of course I had already discovered most of my allergens, but was at such a low physical ebb that I was reacting to just about everything. I believe that the EPD vaccine built up my immune system, thereby raising my allergy tolerance level so that my body was then able to accept a much wider range of foods. After several months of treatment and avoiding the foods which caused the worst reactions, I was able to dispense with this treatment. I am convinced that this boost to my immune system, coupled with the discovery that high daily doses of vitamins kept me in good health, is the reason I have stayed well ever since. This treatment has now been taken up by several other doctors.

Intradermal Skin Tests and Neutralisation
These tests are the most common form of diagnosis used by clinical ecologists. Each food or inhalant is tested individually by injection over a range of strengths to ascertain at which point, if any, the patient reacts. An additional benefit of this testing is that, having established the patient's neutralising point, drops can be made up so that, with proper use, the patient will be able to tolerate an offending allergen without ill effect.

The disadvantage is that from time to time people's

neutralising point changes owing to the ever-fluctuating body chemistry of the allergy sufferer. The strength of the drops then needs to be altered. Nevertheless, of the large number of people who have been given this treatment, the great majority find it successful.

Cytotoxic Blood Test

A programme was shown on television some years ago of the American actor James Coburn having conquered his arthritis through this test, which had been able to identify his food allergies. We were all impatient for it to become available in Britain. When eventually it did, many people asked me where they could get it done. In medically qualified hands I understand this test has been found to be helpful although few people have reported to me that they have benefited. I have, however, heard from many people who were confused or distressed at the vast number of foods to which they were said to be allergic. Subsequent testing on an individual basis has sometimes shown up very different results.

The Prick Test and the RAST Test

These are used by conventional allergists to discover allergies to house dust, pollens, etc. and are fairly reliable when used for this purpose. For food testing they are very limited in range, and are not considered by many doctors to be reliable.

I was given the prick test some years ago after I had fully established that I reacted severely to certain foods. On one arm I was tested for dust, pollens, etc. (which I knew produced only minor symptoms), and most of my arm became red, itchy and interesting. On the other arm I was tested for five food allergies, four of which I knew gave me a severe reaction. Absolutely nothing happened.

The desensitising treatment following prick testing is believed by some doctors to involve possible dangers.

Homoeopathy

I once had the opportunity of talking to a leading homoeopathic pharmacist who had come to give a talk to the members of our allergy group. We came to the mutual conclusion that it seemed highly probable that many people suffering from allergy-induced symptoms were being successfully treated by homoeopathic doctors, even though neither of them might recognise that allergies entered into it. As it is the policy of homoeopathic doctors to treat the whole body as well as giving relief to the symptoms, this form of treatment would seem to give an allergic person the chance to build up his or her strength and so minimise the chance of further allergies developing.

Hair Testing and Non-Medically Accepted Blood Tests

At present there is nothing to stop anyone from setting up an allergy clinic or even calling him or herself a clinical ecologist. This is very misleading to a vulnerable public. These so-called allergy clinics run by non-medically qualified personnel claim to test for allergies by requesting a sample of blood or hair. They sometimes use a form of testing known as radionics which means testing by dangling a pendulum. If it swings one way it denotes allergy, if it swings the other, it denotes the absence of allergy.

In my opinion there is no possible way this can show up a person's allergens. In addition to this, there is nothing in a hair sample which can scientifically show up anything other than the relative quantities of trace minerals in the body, and even this analysis would have to be carried out by someone fully trained in the technique.

Muscle Testing

Muscle testing, otherwise known as applied kinesiology, involves testing the muscles after a solution of allergen is put under the tongue, or even on the tummy, to see if the strength of the muscles has weakened.

Just for fun and in the interest of research, I telephoned a woman advertising allergy testing. I gave details of my symptoms (may I be forgiven) and was asked to bring a sample of all the foods and drinks I take, as individual ingredients. I ascertained that these were to be put individually on my tummy and with each food my muscles would be tested. Her list of qualifications was impressive and I was given every encouragement regarding my recovery.

There is no doubt that *some* allergic reactions after *consuming* food do cause muscle weakness which could show up on a sublingual test, but this is very different from having suspect foods balanced on your navel. In any case, muscle weakness is only one of many possible symptoms. As the great majority of reactions are not immediate anyway, I cannot regard this form of testing as remotely credible.

WHAT TO DO ABOUT YOUR ALLERGIES

The Immune System

The two most important factors in stabilising allergic illness are discovering and avoiding — or being desensitised against — your allergens, and building up your resistance.

As a person's allergic threshold goes hand in hand with their general state of health, the obvious answer is for that person to reach their full health potential.

When allergic people go on to megavitamin therapy, they find this builds up their strength, and thus the severity of their reactions lessens. This continues until they can be said to be stabilised. A few unfortunate severe multiple-allergy sufferers are unable to tolerate vitamins even in their pure form, but these can sometimes be administered by injection.

I started experimenting with vitamins many years ago when I was at a particularly low ebb, in spite of having discovered and eliminated my allergens. I started not with any great expectations, but in sheer desperation. To my amazement and delight, I started looking and feeling considerably better in just under a week. I found other people were interested, and many found that they too benefitted, although some reacted to the ingredients of certain vitamins.

I must emphasise that, although I bought high dosage vitamins, I never exceeded the given dose. Overdosing with vitamins can cause serious physical harm, particularly with vitamins A, D and E, which are fat-soluble and therefore stored in the body.

Many people have of course known for years of the restorative effects of vitamins and I must admit I never took them seriously. It is easy to be sceptical of other people's efforts to get or stay well when you yourself are well without even trying.

Other important factors in building up the immune system and maintaining good health are:

— Eating regularly and well. Sometimes allergic people (especially those suffering from low blood sugar) need to eat small meals more frequently, but everyone needs a basic three good meals a day.

— Fresh air and exercise on a daily basis are essential for keeping fit.

— A proper amount of sleep is necessary for everyone. Young people may be able to burn the candle at both ends — for a limited period — but most of us need a regular, basic eight hours.

Any form of therapy such as meditation, yoga or relaxation may be helpful to some people. Others find a more active pastime, a sport perhaps, of therapeutic value. Breathing exercises can be beneficial, especially to asthmatics. It is important for everyone to know how to breathe properly.

To sum up, give yourself the best chance of staying well by avoiding every type of stress as much as possible, and living a healthy life within your own limitations. This way you will have every chance of stabilising your condition. In time you will gain confidence and lose the fear of always expecting an allergic reaction. Taking the necessary precautions will become second nature and you (and others) will come to accept yourself as a 'normal' person.

Vitamins

The conception, popular among many members of the medical profession, that we all get enough vitamins in our diet does not take into account several important things:

— The highly refined and processed foods around today.

— The increased amount of vitamins required when people are in poor health or under stress.

— That heating and cooking destroy many natural vitamins.

— That some of us have a much higher requirement than others.

The B vitamins have been known for years to be good for 'the nerves'. Therefore, whilst they are helpful to all allergy sufferers, they are particularly beneficial to those who suffer from stressful, psychological allergy-induced symptoms. B vitamins should always be taken in a balanced complex unless otherwise prescribed by someone qualified to do so.

Vitamin C is invaluable in minimising the symptoms of colds and other infections. Before I found out about its beneficial qualities, I used to retire to bed for a couple of days every time I caught a cold because I felt so ill. Now I find I seldom catch one, but if I do the symptoms are now no more than a nuisance.

Vitamic C taken naturally via our diet is depleted through infections and through taking antibiotics, and it is at these times that taking extra is especially valuable. I know a chemist who gives his staff one gramme of vitamin C daily throughout the winter, and they are almost never off sick.

Vitamin C is also a natural antihistamine, and will help to prevent and relieve adverse reactions as well as building up the immune system.

Vitamins B and C are water soluble and so the body eliminates any excess over and above the amount it requires.

Vitamin E helps to replace the natural oils in one's body and is therefore especially good for women over the age of forty, as it helps to keep their skin fresh and supple. It has excellent healing powers when used externally on wounds and burns.

Trace Minerals

Many allergic people seem to be lacking in iron. If you are actually anaemic, it can be prescribed by your doctor in the form of Sytron, which is iron in its natural form with no additives.

Magnesium is a mineral in which allergic people are often deficient, and for those who require extra calcium as well (such as milk-allergic people) this can be bought in the form of dolomite, which is calcium and magnesium combined.

Zinc is recommended by the Hyperactive Children's Support Group, which has often found hyperactive children to be in short supply of this mineral. I believe other allergic people may require it too. It has been known for those who have lost their sense of taste and smell to recover these after taking zinc in the appropriate amount.

Selenium is another mineral that some allergic people claim helps their condition.

Other Supplements

Oil of Evening Primrose is said to have a calming effect on hyperactive children and to be beneficial to women suffering from PMT. It has been tested on children with eczema and a significant improvement was noted. It is also being used to treat arthritis.

Propolis, taken from the hives of bees, was recommended to me some years ago by a woman suffering from allergies who found her health improved after taking it. I have not tried it myself, but I have read that it is recognised as a treatment for wounds and sore throats, and is considered likely to be effective in controlling arthritis.

All vitamins and trace minerals are excellent for building up health if they can be tolerated, but it must be remembered that sensitive people may well be adversely affected either by the vitamins themselves or, more likely, by the materials in which they are based.

One firm which markets vitamins and trace minerals in their purest form is:

Cantassium Company Limited (Larkhall Laboratories),
225 Putney Bridge Road,
London SW15 2PY.

They produce a good multi-vitamin for children called Junamac, and one called Mini Junamac for babies after weaning. Their products can be obtained direct from the above address, from some health food shops, and from certain chemists. Their prices are reasonable, too. Watch out for some other brands of pure vitamins, the costs of which may be quite outrageous.

Water

There is no substitute for water, and allergic people in particular should drink plenty of it. Kettles should always be filled from the cold tap. For those unfortunate people who cannot tolerate tap water, water purifiers can be bought to filter your own water supply. Two such makes are Mayrei and Brita, and these can be bought from health food shops and some hardware shops.

Tap water frequently contains recycled sewage water, which has been treated until it is considered sterile. Small residues in the form of agricultural pollution, industrial discharges and artificial chemicals may all be present in drinking water in amounts too small to be considered a danger to health — except where allergies are concerned. Where water is taken from rivers, traces of detergent may also be found.

Chlorine is added to all water as a safeguard, and in some areas fluoride is added too. People can be adversely affected by either of these chemicals, and a water filter (such as one of the two mentioned above) will remove these and any other harmful chemicals present in your water supply. Two weeks of using bottled water only (for cooking purposes too) will help to clarify whether water is your particular problem before investing in a purifier.

The National Pure Water Association has fought for many years against the compulsory fluoridation of water. It contends that, whereas chlorine and other chemicals are used to treat the water and make it safe to drink, fluoride is added to treat the water *consumer* and is an unacceptable infringement of the fundamental human right to decide for ourselves what substances (intended to affect the development of our bodies) go into our bodies.

Further information can be obtained from the Secretary, Mr N. Brugge, Bank Farm, Aston Pigott, Westbury, Shrewsbury SY5 9HH.

Bread

Remember that the ingredients of everything made outside the home need to be checked. At best, bread is likely to contain wheat, yeast, sugar, salt and an emulsifier (the emulsifier provides chemically what used to be done by kneading). Although 100% wholemeal bread is without doubt the most nutritious, those people who cannot take bran will react to it, and I have actually met some who can tolerate white bread (even with its bleached flour) but not wholemeal.

Salt

It took me quite a while to work out what was making me ill on one occasion. I discovered it was the sodium hexacyanoferrate II put into salt as a pouring agent. I imagine this may apply to other allergic people, so be warned. Sea salt is salt in its pure form; some people seem to be affected even by this. Some doctors believe that salt causes high blood pressure in susceptible people.

Food Substitutes

I have made a list of possible food and drink substitutes, all of which are available either at supermarkets or health food shops. I should like to emphasise that these are only suggested alternatives and should be checked for ingredients and tested on an individual basis before being considered 'safe'.

Common Foods	Possible Substitutes
Cows' milk	Soya, goats' or ewes' milk
Butter	Vegetable or soya margarines Blueband margarine
White sugar	Unrefined or demerara sugar Barbados sugar, honey or molasses Glucose, fructose, dextrose
Wheat flour	Gluten-free flour, rice flour, cornflour, potato flour, rye flour
Meat	Soya meat, pulses, nuts
Lard	Olive oil, sunflower oil, safflower oil

Coffee	Decaffeinated coffee, Barley Cup, dandelion coffee
Tea	Luaka tea, herb teas, Rooibosch tea
Chocolate	Carob (in bars or as powder)
Squashes, fizzy drinks	Pure fruit juices without artificial additives

Diets — General

We hear a great deal these days of the dangers of do-it-yourself diets. Of course, diets *can* be dangerous — so can crossing the road. It depends on how you set about it.

What we do not hear about are the dangers of continuing with a diet which contains food or chemicals to which people are sensitive. Any food intolerance — for whatever reason — will poison your system and continue to do so until you remove it. This is not only distressing, but detrimental to your general state of health. The wonderful thing about our bodies is their excellent regenerative powers, and so, when you remove your allergens, you can get well again, regardless of age.

Never allow any non-medically qualified person to put you (or your child) on to a limited diet for longer than two weeks. Some horrific stories have emerged about people who have been put on prolonged elimination diets; this can be very dangerous in the wrong hands, apart from being totally unnecessary.

We once had a man who came to one of our meetings who had visited a non-medical allergy clinic and had been put on to a very unbalanced diet for *seventeen weeks*. Needless to say, he had lost a lot of weight, felt dreadful, and had paid heavily for the privilege. We often get asked for specific diets (a 'migraine diet' or an 'arthritis diet'). Contrary to what you may read elsewhere, as far as allergy is concerned, there is *no such thing* as a specific diet. People can often have very different reactions to the same food. You might get a headache from eating an orange; I might come out in a rash. People can have the same reaction to different foods. You might get arthritis from eating wheat; I might get arthritis from drinking milk. You may get different reactions to different foods, or the same symptoms with different foods. Everyone is an individual.

There is only one diet and that is the one which is *right for you*.

Nalcrom

Nalcrom (sodium cromoglycate) is now being prescribed by some general practitioners as a food allergy blocking agent for occasional use (e.g. high days and holidays). The majority of people can take it and find it effective, although a few react the first time they try it. Three or four capsules should work, though the gelatine casing is best avoided. Open it up and dissolve the contents in a small amount of very hot (but not boiling) water. In severe cases empty one capsule under the tongue at the same time, and leave the contents there until they dissolve.

This must be taken not less than fifteen minutes before eating, and will be effective for several hours. It is considered safe as it is not absorbed into the blood stream and is eliminated through the body in due course.

Nalcrom does not appear to work as well for liquids as it does for solids, and it does not seem to protect one from a reaction to artificial additives. It should not be taken on an indefinite basis as an allergic person could easily become sensitised to it.

Sodium cromoglycate is also produced in the form of Intal for asthma, Rynacrom and Lomusol for allergic rhinitis, and Opticrom for allergies affecting the eyes. It is a valuable and safe drug prescribed as a preventative, and many allergic people have benefited from it.

Tranquillisers

Coming off tranquillisers is an important part of recovery in allergic illness. Clinical ecologists will get patients to cut down or cut out tranquillisers and other drugs before putting them on to an elimination diet. Alas we have no authority to do this, but hopefully the patient will lose the need for them after allergens have been discovered and eliminated and confidence has been regained.

Moving House

Sometimes people are so allergic in their present environment that they feel it advisable to move house in the hope of improving their health. In these circumstances, it is very important they do not jump out of the frying pan into the fire. The following comments are worth taking into consideration, though trying to follow them all would probably be impracticable.

— Try to live at least five miles away from any factory, to avoid excessive pollutants.

— Whenever possible avoid a house near main roads and roads with parking meters, because of exhaust fumes.

— Fields produce moulds, grass pollen, etc. so it is better not to live too close to them. Also they are treated with pesticides and fertilisers.

— Avoid a house with large trees in the garden or nearby, especially pine trees which are a known source of allergen to some people.

— People with breathing problems should particularly try to avoid low-lying land because of dampness.

— If possible, avoid a house with gas fires. Anyone who is already known to be gas-allergic will need an all-electric house.

— Do not buy a house with cavity wall insulation or floors which require polishing, because of the high allergenic properties of the chemicals involved.

— Avoid a house near a nursery garden or any place where spraying may be done, because the droplets of the chemicals involved will be airborne.

ALLERGY AND DOCTORS

Doctors

Anyone who chooses to consult a professional person other than a doctor — say a solicitor or an accountant — may decide after one interview that their personalities are incompatible, and so they will go elsewhere. This is not so with a general practitioner. Either we register before we meet him or her, or it is taken for granted after one appointment that we will do so. This arrangement can be unsatisfactory for both patient and doctor. There is talk of changing the system and of doctors being able to advertise their special interests and choice of treatments, but so far this is not possible.

The National Consumer Council has asked the government to make it easier for patients to change doctors, for doctors' records to be available for inspection by the patient, and for doctors to publish more information about their practices.

Environmental illness often goes unrecognised by many doctors, even when patients have discovered for themselves that they repeatedly become ill in certain situations. For such people, going to visit their doctor can be an ordeal. Their greatest fear is often the fear of offending the doctor, who may explain their symptoms away as 'your age', 'stress', 'over-anxiety' or 'purely psychological' — as the prescription pad is reached for to prescribe yet another tranquilliser. Of course people suffer from stress from time to time, but the patient is usually the first to be aware of this fact! Advice or suitable therapy could then be prescribed; tranquillisers should only ever be a temporary solution.

Of course there are many doctors who are understanding and knowledgeable. I happen to have one myself, and will illustrate this by telling you about my first experience of allergic illness.

I had been feeling unwell for some time with a general feeling of nausea and debility. My husband and I had been invited out to a business dinner and our coffee cups had been refilled into the early hours. On the way home, however, I started feeling rather ill. By the next morning I had recovered sufficiently to cope, and by mid-morning I had tucked up my baby daughter for her morning nap. I sat down for a coffee break. Ten minutes later I did not know what had hit me. I felt incredibly sick, everything went black and I developed violent palpitations. I felt as if I were engulfed in an enormous tidal wave which would crash any minute, crushing my body into eternity. It was by far the most terrifying experience of my life, and I thought I was going to die. I crawled on my knees to the telephone and managed to dial 999. I was amazed that I was still conscious. I also called a friend, and before long she was joined by two ambulancemen and a doctor, who was kind and understanding and diagnosed 'stress'. To my acute embarassment I soon began to feel somewhat better — so they all went home. Since it was lunchtime, my friend kindly made me some egg sandwiches and a cup of coffee before she left.

After about ten minutes the whole sequence of events began again. I could not believe it. Luckily my daughter was still sleeping. Again I struggled to the phone. Back came my two ambulancemen, and this time they took me to the local hospital. 'All relevant tests' were done, with negative results, and I was sent home in disgrace.

The next day I had a further attack. As it was Saturday my husband called the surgery; my own doctor was on holiday and another partner appeared. He said with righteous irritation that he could find nothing physically wrong with me whatsoever. He prescribed a strong tranquilliser and departed. I took one, and temporarily lost the use of my legs.

After a week of dreaded attacks my own doctor returned from holiday. I phoned him. 'There is something awfully wrong with me — please don't say it's psychological', I begged. 'We will explore all the physical possibilities before we consider the psychological ones', he answered. 'Palpitations can sometimes be caused by alcohol, smoking, tea or coffee.' I had given up the first two, so it did not take me long to discover that coffee was the culprit.

How lucky I was to have a doctor who not only believed me but was able to help with the diagnosis as well. But at the time I did not know just how lucky!

Now, years later, having heard over and over again the stories of other people's distressing experiences, I realise how rare was my doctor's approach.

In recent years our Association has received an increasing number of letters from people whose doctors have advised them to write to us. Nevertheless, it is true to say that the great majority are from people complaining of the disparaging, superior, or plain disinterested attitude of their doctors, and this naturally causes them much distress.

What can doctors do who feel that medications are not always the answer, and would like to help their patients find the cause? What can they possibly do in the five to ten minutes allocated to them in an average surgery visit?

They could refer the patient to a private doctor practising clinical ecology — if they happen to know of one. They could refer them to one of the large London teaching hospitals where some doctors are now seriously studying the subject of food and chemically induced illness. But which hospital and which doctor?

Testing for and desensitising to 'accepted' allergens

73

such as pollens and housedust mite can be done on the NHS, but it is now almost impossible to get this done anywhere other than in a hospital, and it is compulsory to wait two hours after every injection in case of a reaction. Allergens such as these are virtually unavoidable and people do need help.

Likewise, people who are hyperallergic (allergic to many substances) usually need professional help.

Alternatively, and for the great majority of patients, they could look in one of the booklets provided free of charge to all doctors (*Pulse* and *Doctor* to name but two), and find the name of an allergy association which in turn can give the name of a suitable doctor should this prove necessary, though again they will be private.

In conclusion, I believe that people should be made aware of the workings of their own bodies and take more responsibility for their health upon themselves. Some already do so and, of course, there are others who, for one reason or another, are unable to do this but even the least able have some observations to offer which a wise doctor takes into account.

If doctor and patient could work as a team combining the doctor's experience and expertise with the patient's self-awareness, this would not only lead to a healthier and happier situation but ease the doctor's case load as well!

Changing Doctors

If you wish to change your doctor, do not do this on impulse. Take your time. First of all consider whom you might ask to take you on. Then decide if the move is practical from the point of view of reaching the new surgery. Think also of the effect on other members of the family. Will they be changing too? If not, is it going to be awkward for them if they remain with the present doctor?

Make enquiries until you find a doctor who can be recommended by more than one person, and preferably one already known to be interested in allergies. Make an appointment, or write and ask if he or she is willing to take you on, explaining why you wish to make the change. No doctor is obliged to do so, and some practices only take patients from what they consider to be their own area.

Having achieved this, you have two options. Either go to your present doctor and say you are leaving, and ask him or her to sign your medical card. Take it to your new doctor for signing, and he or she will send it to the Family Practitioner Committee.

If your present doctor does not agree to this, or if you want to avoid the embarassment of asking, you can send your medical card to the Family Practitioner Committee explaining why you have not obtained a signature, giving the name and address of your new doctor. They will send you a 'waiting slip' and there will be a lapse of about two weeks before they return your medical card, which you then present to your new doctor for signature.

If you have been unable to find a doctor willing to take you on but are determined to leave your present one, you can write to the Family Practitioner Committee explaining the situation and ask to be put on their 'Allocation Scheme'. This is a rotated list of all the doctors in your area, and the one who happens to be at the top of the list is obliged to take you on for a minimum period of three months. He or she will no doubt keep you unless you are considered to be a very difficult patient, in which case he or she is at liberty to hand your name back to the Family Practitioner Committee to be reallocated to the next doctor at the top of the list.

The address and telephone number of the Family Practitioner Committee can be found under the name of your county in your telephone book.

WOMEN, BABIES AND CHILDREN

Women's Problems
Because of the connection between hormones and allergies, more women suffer from allergies than men. This is not, however, to say that men who are allergic cannot have just as severe reactions — they can.

Women suffering from pre-menstrual tension, post-natal depression or menopausal symptoms may already be using their supply of hormones in counteracting hitherto undiagnosed allergies, and therefore have an inadequate supply when they are needed in extra amounts at these special times. If they were able to avoid the food and inhalant allergens which cause the stress symptoms, they might be better able to cope at such times.

Many years ago, when I was seen at St Mary's Hospital by the (then) Chief Consultant of the Allergy Unit, he told me with obvious excitement, 'We only get about ten people a year as badly affected as you'. He asked if he might bring in a colleague to photograph me, and I could think of no adequate reason for refusing his request. Should I smile and look full of the joys, or put on an expression of dire gloom?

He then explained with enthusiasm to another white-coated doctor all the additional symptoms I was going to suffer when I reached 'the change of life' (hot flushes, severe depression, etc.). Not wanting to spoil a lively discussion, I slipped quietly out. I am pleased to say, several years later, that I proved his prognosis totally wrong. I included this little anecdote because I believe it illustrates the strong possibility that if a woman can get herself really fit by accepting the dictates of her own body chemistry, she has every chance of an easy 'change'.

I have met a few women who recognise that they are only susceptible to allergic reactions during one week in four, just before or at the start of menstruating. By this discovery they have managed to minimise the allergic symptoms that their particular allergens would otherwise have caused. The explanation is simply that at this time in their cycle their resistance is lowered. These people have borderline allergies which they are able to keep under control.

Water retention, causing a bloating of the stomach, is an unpleasant and embarrassing symptom which can sometimes make a woman look pregnant when she is not. The symptoms can often be related to food, or even inhalant, allergens.

A major hormone change takes place after a woman conceives. There is a definite connection between hormone change and allergies. Some allergic women say that pregnancy makes them feel on top of the world and others say they feel considerably less well, sometimes very nauseous. Early morning sickness for the first three months is not abnormal as the body adapts to its hormonal changes, but prolonged severe vomiting is. The greatly increased sense of smell that some women experience may cause temporary inhalant sensitivities, which in turn cause the vomiting. Discovering and avoiding these can eliminate the need for drugs.

Of course not all women's gynaecological symptoms are allergy-induced, but some certainly are, and there is no doubt that being aware of your own body chemistry can save you much distress.

Babies
Babies should be breast-fed for as long as possible with the mother checking that no food or drink she is taking is

affecting the baby. One doctor working in this field says that when mothers under his care are unable to breast-feed, he has found that if he removes cows' milk from their diets they are then able to do so.

Cows' milk should be delayed for as long as possible and introduced warily, because it is one of the most potentially allergenic foods. If your baby proves to be unable to tolerate cows' milk, it will thrive far better without it. Although a very useful commodity, the milk of other species was never intended by nature to be taken by humans — only custom dictates this. If your baby is sensitive to cows' milk, it can be replaced with one of the brands of soya milk made especially for babies available from chemists and health food shops. Unfortunately, a small number of babies will react to this too.

Doctor Cant, formerly of the Eczema Research Clinic at St George's Hospital, Tooting, does not recommend goats' or ewes' milk until the baby reaches the age of one, and even then he advises boiling it.

What do you do if your baby proves unable to take cows' or soya milk? Don't despair — this does happen. If you are not already in the hands of a dietition, you will need to visit one — your doctor can refer you. She or he will be able to ensure that your baby is getting a balanced diet with the necessary supplements.

Introducing New Foods

Cereals — particularly wheat, corn and oats — are also possible allergens, so other cereals should be introduced first. Fruit (with the exception of citrus fruits) and vegetables (with the exception of potatoes, peas and beans) are less likely to cause problems and could be introduced even before cereals, preferably fresh (cooked if necessary) and puréed. I am most grateful to Dr Cant for allowing me to include the following excellent weaning advice devised by him and his Research Dietition, Janet Bailes.

Weaning Advice for Babies With or at Risk of Developing Allergic Disease

Most doctors and health visitors believe that breast-feeding is best for babies, especially babies born into families where close relatives (father, mother, brother, sister) suffer from allergic diseases such as eczema, asthma and hayfever. If such babies are exclusively breast fed for at least four months it seems that they are less likely to develop allergic disease themselves. Less is known about the effect of weaning diet, but there is evidence that suggests that later, more gradual introduction of solids may also reduce the risks of developing such diseases. More research is still needed but these guidelines are based on best available evidence.

Demand exclusive breast feeding should be entirely nutritionally adequate until baby is six months old and probably even after that age, provided that:

— Baby is fed often enough. Although babies become very efficient feeders, this may mean more frequent and longer feeds, and will almost certainly mean feeding during the night. Be prepared for this!

— Baby is weighed regularly to check that weight gain remains satisfactory. This is most important.

— You are having a varied diet with plenty of fluids and an adequate vitamin intake. Remember baby may be taking as much as 800 calories per day from you.

— From six months, until full mixed feeding, baby has supplements of iron and vitamins. We suggest (as they are free from artificial colourings) 0.3 mls. Abidec vitamin drops per day and 2.0 mls. Niferex iron supplement per day.

Thus, try to resist pressure to introduce solids until baby is six months old and then it seems sensible to start with foods which are least likely to provoke an allergic reaction, gradually increasing the number of foods given until the baby is having a full and varied diet by about one year of age.

Introduce only one food group at a time, giving it daily for one week before you decide whether it has an adverse effect — such as a red itchy skin rash, or very loose, watery, offensive stools (obviously if there is an immediate reaction such as swelling and redness of lips and face, then abandon that food and try it again in 4-6 months time).

This is the order in which we suggest you introduce foods:

— Milk-free baby rice (check label), mixed with water or expressed milk.

- Puréed root vegetables (potatoes, carrot, parsnip, swede, turnip).

- Puréed fruit (apple, pear, banana but *not* citrus fruits until nine months).

- Other vegetables (peas, beans, lentils, broccoli etc.).

- Other cereals (but *not* wheat until eight months).

- Lamb, turkey, and then the other meats.

- Fish (not until ten months).

- Other milk and milk products not until ten months, unless breast feeding has diminished to less than four feeds per day, in which case a baby milk will be needed (it is probably better to choose a soya formula such as Formula S (Cow and Gate) or Wysoy (Wyeth)). When starting dairy products try yoghurt first, then boiled cows' milk, and if this is tolerated, then all the milk-containing foods can be introduced — Milupa foods, cheese, butter, etc. Note that we do not recommend goats' or ewes' milk — they are unsuitable without considerable modification until one year of age, and even after this they must be boiled.

- Eggs (not until one year).

Take care when using commercially-prepared baby foods — read the labels carefully. The following ingredients all mean *milk* or *egg* and so beware:

Milk, butter, cream, cheese, cheese powder, skimmed milk powder, non-fat milk solids, casein, caseinate, whey, lactalbumin, egg lecithin.

If in any doubt contact your health visitor or doctor —

they can put you in touch with a dietitian if need be.

Remember there are two equally important objectives, firstly to ensure that baby is adequately nourished and growing well, and secondly to lessen the risk that your baby will develop allergic disease.

The number of letters we receive from mothers of babies and young children would seem to indicate that allergic illness is on the increase. I am very concerned that I have heard in recent years from a small number of mothers whose babies are apparently reacting to every new food they try. As I mentioned earlier in this book, I believe the reason is that babies are nurtured in the bodies of mothers who have themselves been subjected to increased pollutants. Low levels of pesticide residues are reported to have been found in breast milk and in the body fat of babies of only five days old. What about all the other possible toxins which are *not* being tested for? And what of the build-up of possible combined toxins?

To give a baby its very best chance of good health, ideally *both* parents should avoid such hazards as alcohol, smoking and drugs (street, medical or self- prescribed) for at least three months before the intended conception. After conception the mother-to-be should spend her pregnancy in the healthiest possible environment, eating a varied diet of pure food. As the first fifty-six days of conception are the most important this means starting as soon as you hope you have conceived, rather than after it has been confirmed.

For further advice on hyper-allergic babies and preconceptual and pregnancy care write, including an s.a.e., to:

Mrs P. Barnes
Foresight, Association for the Promotion of
Preconceptual Care
The Old Vicarage
Church Lane, Whitley, Surrey GU8 5PN

Names of doctors working in this field can also be supplied on request.

Sometimes mothers of young babies feel quite over-whelmed with the responsibility of caring for such small and vulnerable creatures, especially when they do not seem to be thriving as well as they should. Let me try and give you some encouragement. In giving your baby a natural diet of balanced natural foods and trying to make the environment as pure as possible, you are giving him or her the best possible chance to thrive.

If you should lose track at some point and do not know what the baby is reacting to, go back to the diet you were giving at the time when he or she *was* well. This should clear the system and you can retest the new foods, moni-toring each one in turn. If this does not produce a positive result, check that a new possible inhalant allergen has not been introduced — for example gas heating in the colder weather.

Don't forget that babies are prone to infections too, so don't assume that all illness is an allergy. Check with your doctor if you are in doubt.

Although the bad times seem to go on forever, they are just a phase, and as the baby gets older its digestive and immune systems will mature, and it will be better able to stave off allergic reactions.

Read all you can on the subject of allergy, assimilating the parts which you feel are relevant to your child, trust-ing your own powers of observation, and remember that when a young baby cries, this is his or her way of trying to tell you something. Together you will win through.

Children

'A so far unpublished report commissioned by the Gov-ernment from its nutritional advisers at the Department of Health shows that Britain's overweight teenagers are con-suming masses of fatty and sugary foods'. So reported *The Daily Telegraph* at the beginning of April, 1986. It con-tinues, 'Independent dietitions say the report shows that children are storing up future health problems by eating the wrong foods in their developing years.'

Of course this is a very worrying report, but diet is something over which parents do have *some* control — or at least can state their views. What about the health of children *now*? Many childhood complaints are on the increase — particularly eczema and asthma. Asthma now affects one child in ten. Asthmatics require — and receive — rapid medical attention and are given inhalers and other medications to use at the onset of an attack. But how often are parents advised to look for a cause for this distressing allergy? Very seldom, it appears. If this point is discussed at all, it is likely to be the parent who raises it. The usual answer is that there are too many possibilities to make it worth trying. I say it *is* possible to find the cause. It is not always easy and may take time, but there always *is* a cause and it *is* worthwhile persevering until you find it. If you can chat calmly with your child when she or he is well and likely to be responsive, you may find that the child is able to make a useful contribution.

I suffered quite badly from asthma as a child until the age of thirteen. It was generally accepted that it was caused by cold north-east winds. What my family did not know, because I never told them, was that attacks were also triggered by orange squash and some people's dogs.

One of my worst attacks occurred after a journey with my friend's family, sitting in the back of their car next to their dog. I knew this was going to happen but, due to the complex inhibitions of childhood, I never said a word.

If your child suffers from asthma, tummy pains, headaches or any symptoms which can be classified as 'attacks', then you may be able to pinpoint the cause in the following manner. Make a list of everything the child has eaten and drunk, where they have been and what they have been doing in the twenty-four hours previous to the attack. By doing this several times and comparing notes, a common denominator should emerge.

High fevers can accompany other symptoms in allergic reactions, especially in children, but this is relatively rare. Any child who runs a high temperature *must* be seen by a doctor. Only if the temperature cannot be accounted for in any other way should allergy be considered as a very real possibility.

Anyone with a child who has developed chronic symptoms, or whose mental or physical development is causing concern, should consider the possibility of a food or chemical allergy. This particularly applies when no specific reason can be given by the medical profession and/or where there is a family history of allergy.

Children who from time to time suffer from colds, catarrh, sore throats, ear infections or chest complaints have probably picked up a germ from someone at school. However, those who seem to suffer from one or more of these childhood complaints on a continual basis may well be suffering from allergy-induced symptoms.

Sometimes children do not seem to be developing in the way they should, and naturally this is a matter of grave concern to the parents. Occasionally, and tragically, the reason may be due to brain damage or some genetic defect. Even then much can be done if the child can be given help *as early as possible* by people with experience and expertise. You may have to persevere to ensure this comes about.

There have, however, been some cases of mental retardation which have been wrongly diagnosed. We had a couple contact us who were concerned about their young son. They were convinced the diagnosis that he was mentally retarded was incorrect, because up to the age of eighteen months his responses were well within normal limits. It was only gradually over the next twelve months that he had not progressed the way he should. They were also unhappy with the doctor's assurance that the child's loose bowel movements were nothing to worry about. They never failed to attend a meeting, whether it be a talk by a doctor or a general discussion, although they had some distance to travel. They read all they could lay their hands on. They managed to get their son into the hands of a paediatrician with an interest in clinical ecology, and he diagnosed multiple food allergies with a particularly severe allergy to wheat. Put on to the right diet, the child started to respond in accordance with his age. Being an extreme case, he would always have to be careful, but at least he was lucky in his choice of parents.

Inhalant allergens and intolerances to artificial additives must also be taken into account as possible causes of unsatisfactory development in children. There has been undeniable evidence over the last decade that certain artificial additives, particularly the azo and coal tar dyes, have played a major role where hyperactivity in children is concerned. It is essential that the cause for hyperactivity in each individual be found. The poor child suffers twice over: firstly because a chemical imbalance is causing uncontrollable behaviour and secondly because he or she is getting into trouble for it. Today's undiagnosed hyperactive child can grow in tomorrow's juvenile delinquent.

It was reported in *The Daily Telegraph* on November 12, 1986, that 'A major research study involving 800,000 New York pupils found that their academic achievements improved dramatically when they were given a balanced, nutritious diet and food high in sugar, colouring, preservatives and artificial additives were removed.'

Children's Elimination Diet

To discover which food or foods your child is allergic to, you can put him or her on to the following elimination diet, remembering to remove all possible inhalant allergens at the same time. All the advice given in the section on the adult's elimination diet (page 50) is relevant with the exception of the use of Epsom salts and potassium bicarbonate, which should be omitted as they are too potent for a young person. Allergic children often have poor appetites. A noticeable improvement can occur when allergens have been eliminated. This may be due to an increased sense of taste or smell, or to the loss of a feeling of nausea.

The elimination diet is as follows:

Fresh meat (with the exception of pork)

Fresh fruit (with the exception of citrus fruits)

Fresh vegetables (with the exception of peas and beans and potatoes)

Bottled water from a glass bottle (e.g. Perrier or Malvern Water)

Pure juices made from the above fruits and vegetables

The elimination diet should be given for at least five days, but no more than a week, during which time the child might be difficult as this is the hangover or withdrawal period. When the symptoms have cleared, new foods can be introduced as instructed for adults.

It must be realised that anyone can be allergic to anything, and therefore the above diet is not guaranteed to prove allergy-free for every child, but it will certainly help the majority and hopefully clarify any remaining allergens for those children whose symptoms do not totally clear. A school holiday is the best time to try the elimination diet, for obvious reasons. School lunches may still be a source of colourings and other artificial additives, and allergic children will need to take carefully-planned packed lunches. If head teachers are not responsive to this need, it is to be hoped that you have an enlightened doctor who will agree to send a note.

Going on a diet is not easy, as anyone who has tried it will know. A bit of healthy bribery with star charts and prizes can work wonders. For an older child it could be made into a game called 'Find the Culprit', something along the lines of 'Cluedo'. Anything which achieves results is worthwhile, as the future may depend upon the outcome.

With family support your child should be able to discover his or her allergens and gain in strength. By the time he or she grows older, there is every chance of having the allergies well under control.

Supplementary Benefit and Additive-free Diets

Melanie Miller of the London Food Commission kindly put me in touch with the Child Poverty Action Group, who have supplied the following advice for people with allergic children who are on Supplementary Benefit or Housing Benefit Supplement. If you are in this situation and your child needs an additive-free diet, it may be possible to gain extra supplementary benefits in the form of a 'diet addition' to your weekly benefit to cover the cost of the special diet. Although the DHSS often only awards a small addition initially, the rules do allow an addition to cover the whole cost of the special diet under certain circumstances. Some parents of allergic children have gained as much as £10 per week — often after appealing against an initial refusal.

Ruth Cohen, formerly of C.P.A.G., points out that these payments will be available up until April 1988 (when they will be abolished under the Social Security Act of 1986).

It is well worth claiming the addition even though it will be abolished, as it may help safeguard your benefit level after April 1988. She recommends people wishing to make a claim go to their local welfare rights adviser, Citizens Advice Bureau, or other advice centre, as the rules are quite complicated. If people have considerable problems, their welfare benefit adviser may contact:

C.P.A.G.
4th Floor
1-5 Bath Street
London EC1 V9PY.

Mother's Instinct

Unfortunately the valuable asset of a mother's instinct is usually highly underestimated. This is not surprising when you consider that few men understand the workings of a woman's mind, and that most doctors are men.

This instinct is not some imagined, nebulous, mystical feeling. Rather, it is based on the very strong bond between mother and child endowed by nature for the protection of the species. Added to this, a mother (for whom the child's welfare is paramount) is constantly and closely observing her child's development, and commits to memory all the relevant factors involved, thereby putting two and two together and making four.

Sadly, most doctors are not taught to take mothers' observations into account, as I learned to my son's detriment when he was young. At one period he suffered from continual bronchitis. The doctor diagnosed bronchitis, my son was given an antibiotic, recovered, and had two weeks respite before the pattern was repeated. He sometimes preceeded this illness with a febrile convulsion (caused by a rapid rise in temperature due to the infection coming on too suddenly for the child's body to be able to cope with it). I observed that these attacks were always recognisable in the initial stages because he would be restless in bed, grind his teeth, and develop dark circles under his eyes — *every time*. In the mind of the doctor we had at that time, these were not symptoms but simply a mother's imaginings. Nothing could be heard through the stethoscope therefore the chest *must* be clear. If the chest was clear, there could be no illness. The poor child had to suffer a convulsion before the doctor accepted that he had started yet another attack.

I once heard a paediatrician speaking on TV. I do not recall who he was, but he said, 'Mothers come to me for one of two reasons. Either they ask, "Is my child sick?" in which case I may be able to reassure them (or not, as the case may be). Or they say, "My child *is* sick", in which case they must always be taken seriously.'

How wise he was, and how sad that all doctors are not like him.

COT DEATHS AND RESEARCH

Cot Deaths

I believe that those cot deaths which cannot be accounted for may well be due to severe allergic reactions when foods are introduced for the first time (or for the second time when antibodies have formed from the first intake). I base this hypothesis on the following grounds:

— Even the most orthodox doctors accept that a certain percentage of the population is born predisposed to allergic reaction.

— Babies are particularly vulnerable due to their immature digestive and immune systems.

— Allergic reactions which cause anaphylactic shock can come on rapidly, be severe, and disappear the same way, leaving no trace of symptoms in their wake.

— One manifestation of allergy is swelling. It does not take much swelling temporarily to close a baby's air passages and thus cause suffocation. In these circumstances, the reaction would not even need to culminate in anaphylactic shock for death to occur.

If these facts could be proved to be the cause of cot deaths, then many such deaths could be avoided by the following measures:

91

— Breast-feeding for as long as possible.

— Introducing the least potentially allergenic foods first.

— Introducing new foods only when baby is 100% well.

— Checking for reactions when introducing new foods, especially where cows' milk is concerned.

Research Into Cot Deaths

About 1,500 babies in Britain die suddenly, without explanation, each year.

Although research into allergy as a possible cause has been done, I do not believe it has been done in sufficient detail. Cows' milk and house dust mite have been studied as possible allergens, but very few others. To make a study of allergy valid, I believe the whole spectrum of possible allergens with which a baby might come into contact — including inhalant ones — would have to be studied in conjunction.

The idea that cot deaths might be due to an allergy to cows' milk was propounded in the 1960s. Interest was lost in this hypothesis when it was realised that totally breast-fed babies died from cot deaths too. What they do not seem to have considered is the possibility that the common denominator was *allergy* rather than cows' milk — a *variety* of allergens, differing in each case, manifesting themselves only when a particular solid was first introduced.

Some further studies have been done on parents — sometimes mothers only (why not fathers?) — to find out whether they have a history of what are termed atopic disorders, such as asthma and eczema. What about all the other symptoms implicated in allergy?

It has been questioned as to whether a cot death baby could have been allergic to a virus or other microorganism capable of triggering an allergic reaction. Testing for allergic reactions to viruses, cows' milk and house dust mite is a very limited field. How about tests being done on all the other potentially allergenic foods being introduced for the first time?

I should also be interested to learn whether the increase in cot deaths coincides with the introduction of hormones and antibiotics with which cows are treated nowadays, which find their way into the milk. Fodder is likewise treated with pesticides and fertilisers. Do we really expect none of these things to affect human metabolism?

Research

Research into allergies is really a double issue. Firstly, there is the need for the more far-sighted doctors to convince the 'conventional' allergists that there is already a vast number of people suffering from allergies — both ingested and inhaled — and the numbers are steadily growing.

Quite why some doctors still need convincing, I am not sure. The evidence is there for all to read, at least as far as food allergy is concerned, and chemical allergy is simply a logical extension.

— Double blind trials relating to food allergy and providing conclusive results have been published in the *Lancet* and other medical journals over the past few years.

— Some of the major hospitals in London and elsewhere are already testing people for food allergies, though inevitably only a very small percentage of those who require help. The average GP is unaware of this facility.

— The Report of the Royal College of Physicians and the British Nutrition Foundation gave information in 1984 on the role of food and drink in cases of allergy. Now, four years later, there is no sign of this being officially incorporated into medical training or becoming official medical practice.

Secondly, when it is established that food and chemical allergies actually exist, the next step must be to find the common denominator in multiple allergy sufferers, so that a simple test can be devised to show to what degree a person is affected, and thus what treatment is required.

Scientific tests have to be very precise. The permutations and combinations of the body chemistry of the severely allergic person are infinite. Everything which happens to him or her causes an interaction of constantly fluctuating body chemicals. A reaction may be to a single substance or to any variety or combination of several substances. Chemically speaking, the allergy sufferer is never the same person from one day to the next, even from one hour to the next. For this reason I believe that research will prove complex, if not well-nigh impossible. Can we afford to wait? I say that it is high time that such people were recognised as suffering from a genuine, authentic disease. Let us have recognition first, and explore the whys and wherefores afterwards.

The government appears to hold the complacent and totally erroneous view that sufficient facilities are available on the NHS for allergy sufferers, that the numbers are relatively small, and that food intolerance is well recognised in this country. Until they get their facts straight and act on them, private clinical ecologists will continue to increase their charges, bogus clinics will continue conning the innocent public, and people unable to help themselves will go on suffering unnecessarily.

I quote from a reply to a letter I addressed to Edwina Currie, sent via my MP. It was, in fact, answered by The Baroness Trumpington, Under Secretary of State at the

DHSS, sent to my MP and forwarded to me. It is dated February 18th, 1987.

'There is no doubt about the importance of a nutritious and correctly-balanced diet in promoting and maintaining good health. But I could not go along with the view that a large amount of chronic ill-health was being caused by allergic reactions to chemicals in food, water and the environment. While accepting that there is a need for further research in this area, the view of the medical staff in this Department and of my other expert medical advisers is that relatively small numbers of people suffer significant ill-health due to allergic or other intolerant reactions. They also believe there is no evidence that food additives or synthetic chemicals in the environment are a more potent cause of allergic reactions than the naturally-occurring chemicals in food and other products. Indeed, in the case of foods, there is good evidence that intolerant reactions to natural components of foods are much commoner than reactions to food additives. Of course I accept that for some people allergy may be a cause of much ill-health and suffering, and these unfortunate patients need to have their condition diagnosed and treated to as high a standard as is possible.

'There are 44 allergy clinics in the NHS located in various parts of the country where large numbers of patients have received treatment to relieve or cure their allergies. Many substances causing allergies are widespread and the people affected react to them in different patterns. NHS allergy clinics are equipped to investigate the cause of allergic reaction in individual cases. Diagnosis and treatment of individual cases must be matters for the clinical judgement of the responsible medical practitioners . . . Food intolerance is well recognised and treated within the NHS.'

About nine months, after we started our Association, we conducted our own 'research' by asking for the co-operation of members at one of our regular meetings.

Among the thirty or so who attended, twenty professed to know those foods to which they were allergic. They agreed to fill in forms on which headings of eight common food allergens had been typed. The results were collated and recorded. What I find so fascinating is, that now, twelve years later, that summary still represents a very good synopsis of the symptoms which are so typical of allergy sufferers.

Summary of Symptoms suffered by a random group of twenty members of The Food Allergy Association, June, 1977.

Alcohol — 7

Palpitations, symptoms of drunkenness after minute amount. Sweating, painful muscles, *fatigue*, *depression*, feeling very hot, *headache*, confused, bleeding in stools, indigestion, diarrhoea.

Coffee — 9

chest pains, *palpitations*, dizziness, *fatigue*, *headache*, other aches and pains, insomnia, diarrhoea, irritability, *depression*, nervousness, confusion.

Tea — 3

sweating, indigestion, *depression*, *fatigue*, *palpitations*, eczema, aches and pains, general feeling of being unwell, pruritis, *headache*.

Milk — 5

migraine, *palpitations*, pain in kidneys, sweating, diarrhoea, swelling, indigestion, muscle pains, *fatigue*, *depression*, shaking, unpleasant taste, constipation, frequency.

Wheat — 9

aches and pains, *palpitations*, *fatigue*, *irritability*, *depression*, confusion, sweating, muscle pains, high pulse, breathlessness, lack of co-ordination, nausea, stomach pains, swelling, anxiety, halitosis, eczema, frequency.

Sugar — 7

addiction, indigestion, loss of gain of appetite, gum disease, fainting, convulsions, *depression*, aggression, shaking, tingling, diarrhoea, unable to walk or talk, cystitis, bleeding in stools, rash.

Eggs — 6

Palpitations, fainting, nausea, *headache*, *migraine*, swelling, aggression, *depression*, *fatigue*, diarrhoea, general feeling of being unwell.

Pork — 5

migraine, *headache*, aches and pains, aggression, *depression*, indigestion, tingling, chest pains, diarrhoea, general feeling of being unwell, swollen eyelids, catarrh, *fatigue*.

Of all the common allergens listed above, coffee and wheat predominated, nine out of twenty of the participants being affected in each case. The most common symptoms were: palpitations (six allergens), depression (eight allergens), fatigue (seven allergens), and headaches/migraine (six allergens).

IN CONCLUSION

Had I known when I was a young mother what I know now, I could have saved my own children much unnecessary illness.

What I have learned can help those people who want to be helped and who understand the principles involved. Not everyone does understand, however, and some do not want to know, like the litte old lady who made the classic remark, 'I have had to give up so much since developing rheumatoid arthritis, I'm not going to give up my food as well'. Sadly, there is no help for people like her.

All suffering is distressing, perhaps the greatest of all being the anguish and isolation of acute depression and the terror which may accompany it. Remember, you are not alone. Get in touch with an association. The people who run it will help you to find the cause. They understand and, above all, they care.

ALLERGY ASSOCIATIONS

Everyone running or working in close contact with any sort of self-help group works hard and expends a great deal of both time and energy. This applies to all those in the following associations for allergy-related illness, but I feel two in particular deserve special mention.

Action Against Allergy
Mrs Amelia Nathan-Hill started this association in 1977. I have never personally known anyone who has achieved so much single-handedly. Continually fighting indifferent health, she manages to travel the world promoting an understanding of allergy, putting doctors in touch with one another and helping allergy sufferers wherever she goes. She has organised many symposiums which have given help and hope to thousands of people.

In spite of being away so frequently, she still manages to keep tabs on her London-based association, Action Against Allergy, which has now reached international proportions, having several branches abroad as well as many around Britain.

Hyperactive Childrens' Support Group
Mrs Sally Bundây also started her association in 1977, and she and her mother Mrs Colquhoun devote all of their spare time to helping families with the very distressing problems of living with a hyperactive child. The association has organised conferences in London which have been attended by many people from all round the country, with experienced speakers and some knowledgeable doctors from both Britain and abroad.

HCSG now employs staff to answer the thousands of letters they receive. They have been influential in seeking to cut out those artificial colours which produce devastating effects on those people who are sensitive to them.

Since they have proved that even the most severe cases of hyperactivity can be controlled when the causative toxins are removed, they now have a good deal of medical support. They have kept up their determined efforts, despite fighting at least initially against all odds, and I have the greatest admiration for all they have achieved.

Associations to Help Multiple Allergy Sufferers

Action Against Allergy (Mrs A. Nathan-Hill)
43 The Downs,
London SW20 8HG
Tel: 01 947 5082

Books available on all
types of allergy-based
conditions.

Airedale Support Group (Mrs J. Wilson-Storey)
Briar Lea,
Brookhouse,
Nr. Laughton,
Sheffield S31 7YA.
Tel: Dinnington 567929 (Ring preferably evenings and
weekends)

Allergy Support Group, Oxford (Mrs V. Hibbert)
Lord's Cottage, 20 Queen Street,
Eynsham, Oxon OX8 1HQ
Tel: Oxford 883708 (Ring preferably between 4 and
6 p.m.)

Cambridge Food Intolerance Society (Mrs K. Faruqi)
3 Stearne's Yard,
Haslingfield,
Cambridge CB3 7JA.
Tel: Cambridge 871309

Chemical Victims (Mrs S. Hedges)
12 Highlands Road
Off Old Kempshott Lane,
Basingstoke,
Hants. RG22 5ES.
Tel: Basingstoke 465093

Colchester and District Allergy Group (Mrs D. Rowlinson)
10 Chestnut Avenue,
Blackheath,
Colchester,
Essex CO2 OAL.
Tel: Colchester 577705

Hyperactive Children's Support Group (Mrs S. Bunday)
71 Whyke Lane,
Chichester,
West Sussex.
Tel: Worthing 725182 (Ring between 9.30 a.m. and 3.30 p.m.).

Hythe Food and Chemical Victims' Allergy Club (Mr J.W. Spells)
44 Fairview Drive,
Hythe,
Southampton,
Hants. SO4 5GY
Tel: Hythe 848902

Irish Allergy Treatment and Research Association Ltd.,
PO Box 1067
Churchtown
Dublin 14,
Eire

Levenmouth Allergy Support Group (Mrs E. Wallace)
10 Rannoch Road
Methil
Fife KY8 3JD
Tel: 0333 24247

Lothian Allergy Support Group (Miss J. Sturgeon)
19 Warrender. Park Crescent
Edinburgh 9
(or Tel. Mrs E. Girling on 031 556 6924)

National Society of Research into Allergy (Mrs E.
Rose)
P.O. Box 45
Hinkley,
Leicestershire LE10 1JY.
Tel: Hinkley 635212

Nottingham Food Allergy Support Group (Mrs S.
Footit)
45 Walton Drive,
Keyworth,
Nottingham NG12 5FN.
Tel: Plumtree 4693

Society for Environmental Therapy (Mr A.
Beckingham)
31 Sarah Street,
Darwen,
Lancs. BB3 3ET.

*Scientific Society open to
professionals as well as
the lay public.*

I have not included the name of my own Association in
this list because our advice would be for people to buy this
book. Other associations will provide fresh ideas and
additional information whether or not you happen to live
in their area. They can also put people in touch with
clinical ecologists. The majority have memberships and
regular meetings, which mine does not.

Anti-Allergy Laughing Syndrome.

This book would not be complete without some reference to the Anti-Allergy Laughing Syndrome. This is not uncommon, and many people suffer from it. It has been very fashionable in recent years to find other people's allergies a subject of great amusement.

Take my dentist, for example. When I registered with him some years ago, I thought it a wise precaution to mention I was a very allergic person. This caused him much mirth and, when he had finished laughing, he wrote on my card 'very allergic'. I wonder if any other condition would have warranted those inverted commas?

For the period of time during which I was hyper-allergic, I seldom went out socialising, but if I did I drank water from a wine glass which, I was convinced (though quite mistakenly) fooled everyone. Once at a cocktail party, two well-endowed ladies came up and asked me why I was not eating anything. I explained that I suffered from several food allergies. Looking at my skeletal frame, one gave a great guffaw whilst stuffing smoked salmon, turned to the other and remarked, 'I wish I suffered from a few food allergies.' The other, munching mouthfuls of mince pie, responded with equal enthusiasm.

It is, however, some consolation to those of us who have to contend with second-rate body chemistries, that we can bring fleeting moments of joy to the relatively dull lives of those to whom the word 'allergy' must forever remain an enigma.

OTHER USEFUL ADDRESSES

Foodwatch International
Butts Pond Industrial Estate
Sturminster Newton
Dorset DT10 1AZ
Tel: 0258 73356

This is a mail order service providing a wide range of foodstuffs especially tailored to the needs of allergy sufferers and others requiring special diets. They offer the following services:

— A wide range of unadulterated foods sent by mail order or carrier to any address in the UK or abroad.

— Water purification systems to suit individual needs.

— A Technical Advisory Service on food composition, nutritional values, labelling, etc.

— A Testing Facility (by appointment) for food and environmental allergies and associated problems.

Please send an s.a.e. for further details.

Cotton On
29 N. Clifton Street
Lytham FY8 5HW
Lancs.
Tel: 0253 736611

This is a company producing all-cotton goods and will be invaluable to people for whom wool and/or artificial fibres are a problem. A leaflet illustrating their products will be sent on request.

They produce a wide range of children's clothing in pretty colours and practical styles. This includes beach-wear, underwear, pyjamas, jumpers, dungarees, T- shirts, tights and socks and boys' classic school shirts and trous-ers. For adults they have jumpers, cardigans, stockings and tights. They also do a range of coloured 100% cotton cellular blankets in all sizes. They have a 100% cotton velvet teddy — a lovely idea for those children who are allergic to synthetic materials.

Horn House Hotel
Longformacus
Duns
Berwickshire
Tel: 03617 291

This is a relatively new hotel set in the beautiful Lammer-muir Hills in southern Scotland. The diet and environ-ment have been well researched to provide the safest possible conditions for allergy sufferers in a setting which can also be much enjoyed by the non-allergic members of the family.

The management allows no smoking, perfumes or sprays for the protection of guests who may be sensitive to such things. There is no gas, the water is filtered, and only safe cleaning agents are used. All the upholstery and bedding are made from natural fibres.

Guests can enjoy gluten-free bread, cakes and biscuits and a choice of cows', goats, ewes' or soya milk. Fruit and vegetables are organically grown and the meat is naturally produced.

All diets are catered for and guests will find a quiet, relaxed atmosphere and understanding in all their allergy problems. For further information write or phone for their up-to-date brochure.

A list of further accommodation catering for the needs of allergy sufferers can be obtained (on receipt of an s.a.e.) from chemical victims' member:

> Mrs B. Hardcastle
> 40 Liebenrood Road
> Reading RG3 2EB
> Berkshire

> Norfolk Lavender Ltd.,
> Caley Mill
> Heacham
> Kings Lynn,
> Norfolk PE31 1BR
> Tel: 0485 70384

Norfolk Lavender is the only lavender farm left in England. Their delightful products include fragrances, soaps, bath products and lotions, sachets and dried lavender flowers and pretty Victorian gifts. A royalty is given to registered nature conservation charities — a lovely thought.

Their products are sold in pharmacies and gift shops but they offer a door-to-door mail order service for those who have difficulty in obtaining them. Many people who find they are sensitive to the chemicals used in many commercially produced scented goods will enjoy the pleasure of using these natural products.

WHERE TO BUY ADDITIVE-FREE PRODUCTS

Whilst health food shops must surely be coming into their own as more and more people realise the short and long term hazards of artificial additives, the general stores are not lagging behind.

I wish to give a special mention to Boots, which is a shop I find I am using more than ever before. In their main branches they are stocking some very useful artificial-additive-free foods at competitive prices. Incidentally, they also cater for vegetarian requirements. Particularly useful is their range of preparations for laundering, and a washing-up liquid, all of which are designed for sensitive skins, and are perfume and colour free.

Boots also have a No. 7 unperfumed range of skin care and colour cosmetics, and a fragrance-free version of Boots Skin Kindly products. In addition, Boots' own ranges include toiletries such as moisturisers, cleansers, eye make-up removers, anti-perspirants and hair sprays, and a whole range of colour cosmetics. These are unperfumed and dermatologically tested and should be suitable for sensitive skins. Further details can be obtained from the counter of your local Boots branch.

RECOMMENDED READING

Davies, Gwynne H. *Overcoming Food Allergies* Ashgrove Press, 1985

Eagle, Robert *Eating and Allergy* Thorsons, 1986

Edwards, Linda *Baking for Health* Prism Press, 1986

Grant, Dr Ellen C.G. *The Bitter Pill* Corgi, 1986

Hanssen, Maurice *E for Additives* Thorsons, 1984

Levin, Alan Scott *The Allergy Relief Programme* Gateway Books, 1985

McClure, Clare *Parents' Handbook* Sheldon Press, 1988

Mackarness, Dr Richard *Not All in the Mind* Pan, 1976

Mackarness, Dr Richard *Chemical Victims* Pan, 1980

Mansfield, Dr John *The Migraine Revolution* Thorsons, 1986

Metland, Daphne *A Pocketful of E's* Foulsham, 1986

Mindell, Earl *The Vitamin Bible* Arlington, 1986

Moore, Pauline *Milk-free, Egg-free Recipes for Children* Foulsham, 1986

Mumby, Dr Keith *The Food Allergy Plan* Unwin, 1985

Mumby, Dr Keith *Allergies — What Everyone Should Know* Unwin, 1986

Nathan-Hill, Amelia *Against the Unsuspected Enemy* New Horizon, 1980

Parish, Prof. Peter *Medicines: A Guide for Everybody* Penguin Books, 1987

Rippere, Vicky *The Allergy Problem* Thorsons, 1983

Scott, Sue *Wholefood for the Whole Family* Paperfronts, 1986

Trickett, Shirley A. *Coming Off Tranquillisers* Thorsons, 1986

Webb, Tony and Tim Lang *Food Irradition — The Facts* Thorsons, 1987

Workman, Hunter and Alun Jones *The Allergy Diet* Martin Dunitz, 1984

LIST OF E NUMBERS

To find a particular additive on this list, look first at its category as listed on the label — for example, Colour or Preservative. Additives are listed in numerical order *within* each category. Those without numbers are listed alphabetically at the end of each section. The list also tries to give an idea of foods in which each additive is used. Many additives can be used for similar functions. These additives are listed together. Examples of foods in which they might be used are given at the bottom of each box. The uses given are merely examples — they do not represent the only uses to which the additives are put nor are they meant to imply that these are the only uses allowed by law. The asterisks denote azo or coal tar dyes.

Antioxidants

Stop fatty foods from going rancid and protect fat-soluble vitamins from the harmful effects of oxidation.

E300   **L-ascorbic acid** ■ fruit drinks; also used to improve flour and bread dough
E301   **sodium L-ascorbate** ■
E302   **calcium L-ascorbate** ■
E304   **6-0-pal-mitoyl-L-ascorbic acid (ascorbyl palmitate)** ■ scotch eggs
E306   **extracts of natural origin rich in tocopherols** ■ vegetable oils
E307   **synthetic alpha-tocopherol** ■ cereal-based baby foods
E308   **synthetic gamma-tocopherol** ■
E309   **synthetic delta-tocopherol** ■
E310   **propyl gallate** ■ vegetable oils; chewing gum
E311   **octyl gallate** ■
E312   **dodecyl gallate** ■
E320   **butylated hydroxyanisole (BHA)** ■ beef stock cubes; cheese spread
E321   **butylated hydroxytoluene (BHT)** ■ chewing gum
E322   **lecithins** ■ low fat spreads; also used as an emulsifier in chocolate
      diphenylamine ■
      ethoxyquin ■ used to prevent 'scald' (a discolouration) on apples and pears

Colours

Make food more colourful, compensate for colour lost in processing.

E100   **curcumin** ■ flour confectionery, margarine
E101   **riboflavin** ■ sauces
101(a)   **riboflavin-5′-phosphate** ■
*E102   **tartrazine** ■ soft drinks
*E104   **quinoline yellow** ■
*107   **yellow 2G** ■
*E110   **sunset yellow FCF** ■ biscuits
E120   **cochineal** ■ alcoholic drinks
*E122   **carmoisine** ■ jams and preserves

*E123	**amaranth** ■	
*E124	**ponceau 4R** ■ dessert mixes	
E127	**erythrosine** ■ glacé cherries	
*128	**red 2G** ■ sausages	
*E131	**patent blue V** ■	
*E132	**indigo carmine** ■	
*133	**brilliant blue FCF** ■ canned vegetables	
E140	**chlorophyll** ■	
E141	**copper complexes of chlorophyll and chlorophyllins** ■	
*E142	**green S** ■ pastilles	
E150	**caramel** ■ beer, soft drinks, sauces, gravy browning	
*E151	**black PN** ■	
E153	**carbon black (vegetable carbon)** ■ liquorice	
*E154	**brown FK** ■ kippers	
*E155	**brown HT (chocolate brown HT)** ■ chocolate cake	
160(a)	**alpha-carotene; beta-carotene; gamma-carotene** ■ margarine, soft drinks	
E160(b)	**annatto; bixin; norbixin** ■ crisps	
E160(c)	**capsanthin; capsorubin** ■	
E160(d)	**lycopene** ■	
E160(e)	**beta-apo-8′ carotenal** ■	
E160(f)	**ethyl ester of beta-apo-8′-carotenoic acid** ■	
E161(a)	**flavoxanthin** ■	
E161(b)	**lutein** ■	
E161(c)	**cryptoxanthin** ■	
E161(d)	**rubixanthin** ■	
E161(e)	**violaxanthin** ■	
E161(f)	**rhodoxanthin** ■	
E161(g)	**canthanxanthin** ■	
E162	**beetroot red (betanin)** ■ ice-cream, liquorice	
E163	**anthocyanins** ■ yoghurt	
E171	**titanium dioxide** ■ sweets	
E172	**iron oxides; iron hydroxides** ■	
E173	**aluminium** ■	
E174	**silver** ■	
E175	**gold** ■ cake decorations	
*E180	**pigment rubine (lithol rubine BK)** ■	
	methyl violet ■ used for the surface marking of citrus fruit	
	paprika ■ canned vegetables	
	saffron; crocin ■	
	sandalwood; santolin ■	
	turmeric ■ soups	

Emulsifiers and Stabilisers

Enable oils and fats to mix with water in foods; add to smoothness and creaminess of texture; retard baked goods going stale.

E400	**alginic acid** ■ ice-cream; soft cheese
E401	**sodium alginate** ■ cake mixes
E402	**potassium alginate** ■
E403	**ammonium alginate** ■
E404	**calcium alginate** ■
E405	**propane-1, 2-diol alginate (propylene glycol alginate)** ■ salad dressing; cottage cheese
E406	**agar** ■ ice-cream
E407	**carrageenan** ■ quick setting jelly mixes; milk shakes
E410	**locust bean gum (carob gum)** ■ salad cream
E412	**guar gum** ■ packet soups and meringue mixes
E413	**tragacanth** ■ salad dressings; processed cheese
E414	**gum arabic (acacia)** ■ confectionery
E415	**xanthan gum** ■ sweet pickle; coleslaw
416	**karaya gum** ■ soft cheese; brown sauce
430	**polyoxyethylene (8) stearate** ■
431	**polyoxyethylene (40) stearate** ■
432	**polyoxyethylene (20) sorbitan monolaurate (Polysorbate 20)** ■
433	**polyoxyethylene (20) sorbitan mono-oleate (Polysorbate 80)** ■
434	**polyoxyethylene (20) sorbitan monopalmitate (Polysorbate 40)** ■
435	**polyoxyethylene (20) sorbitan monostearate (Polysorbate 60)** ■
436	**polyoxyethylene (20) sorbitan tristearate (Polysorbate 65)** ■ bakery products; confectionery creams
E440(a)	**pectin** ■
E440(b)	**amidated pectin** ■
	pectin extract ■ jams and preserves
442	**ammonium phosphatides** ■ cocoa and chocolate products
E460	**microcrystalline cellulose; alpha-cellulose (powdered cellulose)** ■ high-fibre bread; grated cheese
E461	**methylcellulose** ■ low fat spreads
E463	**hydroxypropylcellulose** ■
E464	**hydroxypropylmethylcellulose** ■ edible ices
E465	**ethylmethylcellulose** ■ gateaux
E466	**carboxymethylcellulose, sodium salt (CMC)** ■ jelly; gateaux

E470	sodium, potassium and calcium salts of fatty acids ■ cake mixes
E471	mono-and di-glycerides of fatty acids ■ frozen desserts
E472(a)	acetic acid esters of mono- and di-glycerides of fatty acids ■ mousse mixes
E472(b)	lactic acid esters of mono- and di-glycerides of fatty acids ■ dessert topping
E472(c)	citric acid esters of mono- and di-glycerides of fatty acids ■ continental sausages
E472(e)	mono- and diacetyltartaric acid esters of mono- and di-glycerides of fatty acids ■ bread; frozen pizza
E473	sucrose esters of fatty acids ■
E474	sucroglycerides ■ edible ices
E475	polyglycerol esters of fatty acids ■ cakes and gateaux
476	(polyglycerol esters of polycondensed fatty acids of castor oil (polyglycerol polyricinoleate) ■ chocolate-flavour coatings for cakes
E477	propane-1, 2-diol esters of fatty acids ■ instant desserts
478	lactylated fatty acid esters of glycerol and propane-1, 2-diol ■
E481	sodium stearoyl-2-lactylate ■ bread, cakes and biscuits
E482	calcium stearoyl-2-lactylate ■ gravy granules
E483	stearyl tartrate ■
491	sorbitan monostearate ■
492	sorbitan tristearate ■
493	sorbitan monolaurate ■
494	sorbitan mono-oleate ■
494	sorbitan monopalmitate ■ cake mixes
	dioctyl sodium sulphosuccinate ■ used in sugar refining to help crystallisation
	extract of quillaia ■ used in soft drinks to promote foam
	oxidatively polymerised soya bean oil ■
	polyglycerol esters of dimerised fatty acids of soya bean oil ■ emulsions used to grease bakery tins

115

Preservatives

Protect food against microbes which cause spoilage and food poisoning. They also increase storage life of foods.

E200   **sorbic acid** ■ soft drinks; fruit yoghurt; processed cheese slices
E201   **sodium sorbate** ■
E202   **potassium sorbate** ■
E203   **calcium sorbate** ■ frozen pizza; flour confectionery
E210   **benzoic acid** ■
E211   **sodium benzoate** ■
E212   **potassium benzoate** ■
E213   **calcium benzoate** ■
E214   **ethyl 4-hydroxybenzoate (ethyl para-hydroxybenzoate)** ■
E215   **ethyl 4-hydroxybenzoate, sodium salt (sodium ethyl para-hydroxybenzoate)** ■
E216   **propyl 4-hydroxybenzoate (propyl para-hydroxybenzoate)** ■
E217   **propyl 4-hydroxybenzoate, sodium salt (sodium propyl para-hydroxybenzoate)** ■
E218   **methyl 4-hydrobenzoate (methyl para-hydroxybenzoate)** ■
E219   **methyl 4-hydroxybenzoate, sodium salt (sodium methyl para-hydroxybenzoate)** ■ beer, jam, salad cream, soft drinks, fruit pulp, fruit-based pie fillings, marinated herring and mackerel
E220   **sulphur dioxide** ■
E221   **sodium sulphite** ■
E222   **sodium hydrogen sulphite (sodium bisulphite)** ■
E223   **sodium metabisulphite** ■
E224   **potassium metabisulphite** ■
E226   **calcium sulphite** ■
E227   **calcium hydrogen sulphite (calcium bisulphite)** ■ dried fruit, dehydrated vegetables, fruit juices and syrups, sausages, fruit-based dairy desserts, cider, beer and wine; also used to prevent browning of raw peeled potatoes and to condition biscuit doughs
E230   **biphenyl (diphenyl)** ■
E231   **2-hydroxybiphenyl (orthophenylphenol)**
E232   **sodium biphenyl-2-yl oxide (sodium orthophenylphenate)** ■ surface treatment of citrus fruit
E233   **2-(thiazol-4-yl) benzimidazole (thiabendazole)** ■ surface treatment of bananas
234   **nisin** ■ cheese, clotted cream
E239   **hexamine (hexamethylenetetramine)** ■ marinated herring and mackerel

E249	**potassium nitrite** ■
E250	**sodium nitrite** ■
E251	**sodium nitrate** ■
E252	**potassium nitrate** ■ bacon, ham, cured meats, corned beef and some cheeses
E280	**propionic acid** ■
E281	**sodium propionate** ■
E282	**calcium propionate** ■
E283	**potassium propionate** ■ bread and flour confectionery, Christmas pudding

Sweeteners

There are two types of sweeteners — intense sweeteners and bulk sweeteners. Intense sweeteners have a sweetness many times that of sugar and are therefore used at very low levels: they are marked with '*' in the list below. Bulk sweeteners have about the same sweetness as sugar and are used at the same sort of levels as sugar.

	*acesulfame potassium ■ canned foods, soft drinks, table-top sweeteners ■
	*aspartame ■ soft drinks, yoghurts, dessert and drink mixes, sweetening tablets
	hydrogenated glucose syrup isomalt ■
E421	**mannitol** ■ sugar-free confectionery
	*saccharin ■
	*sodium saccharin ■
	*calcium saccharin ■ soft drinks, cider, sweetening tablets, table-top sweeteners ■
E420	**sorbitol; sorbitol syrup** ■ sugar-free confectionery, jams for diabetics
	*thaumatin ■ table-top sweeteners, yoghurt
	xylitol ■ sugar-free chewing gum

Others

Acids, anti-caking agents, anti-foaming agents, bases, buffers, bulking agents, firming agents, flavour modifiers, flour bleaching agents, flour improvers, glazing agents, humectants, liquid freezants, packaging gases, propellants, release agents, sequestrants and solvents.

E170	**calcium carbonate** ■ base, firming agent, release agent, diluent; nutrient in flour
E260	**acetic acid** ■
E261	**potassium acetate** ■
E262	**sodium hydrogen diacetate** ■
262	**sodium acetate** ■ acid/acidity regulators (buffers) used in pickles, salad cream and bread; they contribute to flavour and provide protection against mould growth
E263	**calcium acetate** ■ firming agent; also provides calcium which is useful in quick-set jelly mix
E270	**lactic acid** ■ acid/flavouring protects against mould growth; salad dressing, soft margarine
E290	**carbon dioxide** ■ carbonating agent/packaging gas and propellant; used in fizzy drinks
296	**DL-malic acid; L-malic acid** ■
297	**fumaric acid** ■ acid/flavouring; used in soft drinks, sweets, biscuits, dessert mixes and pie fillings
E325	**sodium lactate** ■ buffer, humectant; used in jams, preserves, sweets, flour confectionery
E326	**potassium lactate** ■ buffer; jams, preserves and jellies
E327	**calcium lactate** ■ buffer, firming agent; canned fruit, pie filling
E330	**citric acid** ■
E331	**sodium dihydrogen citrate (monosodium citrate); disodium citrate; trisodium citrate** ■
E332	**potassium dihydrogen citrate (monopotassium citrate); tripotassium citrate** ■
E333	**monocalcium citrate; dicalcium citrate; tricalcium citrate** ■ acid/flavourings, buffers, sequestrants, emulsifying salts (calcium salts are firming agents); used in soft drinks, jams, preserves, sweets, UHT cream, processed cheese, canned fruit, dessert mixes, ice-cream
E334	**L-(+)-tartaric acid** ■
E335	**monosodium L-(+)-tartrate; disodium L-(+)-tartrate** ■
E336	**monopotassium L-(+)-tartrate (cream of tartar); dipotassium L-(+)-tartrate** ■

E337	**potassium sodium L-(+)-tartrate** ■ acid/flavourings, buffers, emulsifying salts, sequestrants; used in soft drinks, biscuit creams and fillings, sweets, jams, dessert mixes and processed cheese
E338	**orthophosphoric acid (phosphoric acid)** ■ acid/flavourings; soft drinks, cocoa
E339	**sodium dihydrogen orthophosphate; disodium hydrogen orthophosphate; trisodium orthophosphate** ■
E340	**potassium dihydrogen orthophosphate; dipotassium hydrogen orthophosphate; tripotassium orthophosphate** ■ buffers, sequestrants, emulsifying salts; used in dessert mixes, non-dairy creamers, processed cheese
E341	**calcium tetrahydrogen diorthophosphate; calcium hydrogen orthophosphate; tricalcium diorthophosphate** ■ firming agent, anti-caking agent, raising agent; cake mixes, baking powder, dessert mixes
350	**sodium malate; sodium hydrogen malate** ■
351	**potassium malate** ■ buffers, humectants; used in jams, sweets, cakes, biscuits
352	**calcium malate; calcium hydrogen malate** ■ firming agent in processed fruit and vegetables
353	**metatartaric acid** ■ sequestrant used in wine
355	**adipic acid** ■ buffer/flavouring; sweets, synthetic cream desserts
363	**succinic acid** ■ buffer/flavouring; dry foods and beverage mixes
370	**1, 4-heptonolactone** ■ acid, sequestrant; dried soups, instant desserts
375	**nicotinic acid** ■ colour stabiliser and nutrient; bread, flour, breakfast cereals
380	**triammonium citrate** ■ buffer, emulsifying salt; processed cheese
381	**ammonium ferric citrate** ■ dietary iron supplement; bread
385	**calcium disodium ethylenediamine-NNN'N'-tetra-acetate (calcium disodium EDTA)** ■ sequestrant; canned shellfish
E422	**glycerol** ■ humectant, solvent; cake icing, confectionery
E450(a)	**disodium dihydrogen diphosphate; trisodium diphosphate; tetrasodium diphosphate; tetrapotassium diphosphate** ■
E450(b)	**pentasodium triphosphate; pentapotassium triphosphate** ■
E450(c)	**sodium polyphosphates, potassium polyphosphates** ■ buffers, sequestrants, emulsifying salts, stabilisers, texturisers, raising agents; used in whipping cream, fish and meat products, bread, processed cheese, canned vegetables
500	**sodium carbonate; sodium hydrogen carbonate (bicarbonate of soda); sodium sesquicarbonate** ■

501	**potassium carbonate; potassium hydrogen carbonate** ■ bases, aerating agents, diluents; used in jams, jellies, self-raising flour, wine, cocoa
503	**ammonium carbonate; ammonium hydrogen carbonate** ■ buffer, aerating agent; cocoa, biscuits
504	**magnesium carbonate** ■ base, anti-caking agent; wafer biscuits, icing sugar
507	**hydrochloric acid** ■
508	**potassium chloride** ■ gelling agent, salt substitute; table salt replacement
509	**calcium chloride** ■ firming agent in canned fruit and vegetables
510	**ammonium chloride** ■ yeast food in bread
513	**sulphuric acid** ■
514	**sodium sulphate** ■ diluent for colours
515	**potassium sulphate** ■ salt substitute
516	**calcium sulphate** ■ firming agent and yeast food; bread
518	**magnesium sulphate** ■ firming agent
524	**sodium hydroxide** ■ base; cocoa, jams and sweets
525	**potassium hydroxide** ■ base; sweets
526	**calcium hydroxide** ■ firming agent, neutralising agent; sweets
527	**ammonium hydroxide** ■ diluent and solvent for food colours, base; cocoa
528	**magnesium hydroxide** ■ base; sweets
529	**calcium oxide** ■ base; sweets
530	**magnesium oxide** ■ anti-caking agent; cocoa products
535	**sodium ferrocyanide** ■
536	**potassium ferrocyanide** ■ anti-caking agents in salt; crystallisation aids in wine
540	**dicalcium diphosphate** ■ buffer, neutralising agent; cheese
541	**sodium aluminum phosphate** ■ acid, raising agent; cake mixes, self-raising flour, biscuits
542	**edible bone phosphate** ■ anti-caking agent
544	**calcium polyphosphates** ■ emulsifying salt; processed cheese
545	**ammonium polyphosphates** ■ emulsifier, texturiser; frozen chicken
551	**silicon dioxide (silica)** ■ anti-caking agent; skimmed milk powder, sweeteners
552	**calcium silicate** ■ anti-caking agent, release agent; icing sugar, sweets
553(a)	**magnesium silicate synthetic; magnesium trisilicate** ■ anti-caking agent; sugar confectionery
553(b)	**talc** ■ release agent; tabletted confectionery
554	**aluminium sodium silicate** ■
556	**aluminium calcium silicate** ■

558	**bentonite** ∎
559	**kaolin** ∎
570	**stearic acid** ∎ anti-caking agents
572	**magnesium stearate** ∎ emulsifier, release agent; confectionery
575	**D-glucono-1, 5-lactone (glucono delta-lactone)** ∎ acid, sequestrant; cake mixes, continental sausages
576	**sodium gluconate** ∎
577	**potassium gluconate** ∎ sequestrants
578	**calcium gluconate** ∎ buffer, firming agent, sequestrant; jams, dessert mixes
620	**L-glutamic acid** ∎
621	**sodium hydrogen L-glutamate (monosodium glutamate; MSG)** ∎
622	**potassium hydrogen L-glutamate (monopotassium glutamate)** ∎
623	**calcium dihydrogen di-L-glutamate (calcium glutamate)** ∎
627	**guanosine 5'-disodium phosphate (sodium guanylate)** ∎
631	**inosine 5'-disodium phosphate (sodium inosinate)** ∎
635	**sodium 5'-ribonucleotide** ∎ flavour enhancers used in savoury foods and snacks, soups, sauces and meat products
636	**maltol** ∎
637	**ethyl maltol** ∎ flavourings/flavour enhancers used in cakes and biscuits
900	**dimenthylpolysiloxane** ∎ anti-foaming agent
901	**beeswax** ∎
903	**carnauba wax** ∎ glazing agents used in sugar and chocolate confectionery
904	**shellac** ∎ glazing agent used to wax apples
905	**mineral hydrocarbons** ∎ glazing/coating agent used to prevent dried fruit sticking together
907	**refined microcrystalline wax** ∎ release agent; chewing gum
920	**L-cysteine hydrochloride** ∎
924	**potassium bromate** ∎
925	**chlorine** ∎
926	**chlorine dioxide** ∎
927	**azidicarbonamide** ∎ flour treatment agents used to improve the texture of bread, cake and biscuit doughs
	aluminium potassium sulphate ∎ firming agent; chocolate-coated cherries
	2-aminoethanol ∎ base; caustic lye used to peel vegetables
	ammonium dihydrogen orthophosphate; diammonium hydrogen othophosphate ∎ buffer, yeast food
	ammonium sulphate ∎ yeast food
	benzoyl peroxide ∎ bleaching agent in flour
	butyl stearate ∎ release agent

calcium heptonate ■ firming agent, sequestrant; prepared fruit and vegetables

calcium phytate ■ sequestrant; wine

dichlorodifluoromethane ■ propellant and liquid freezant used to freeze food by immersion

diethyl ether ■ solvent

disodium dihydrogen ethylenediamine-NNN'N'-tetra-acetate (disodium dihydrogen EDTA) ■ sequestrant; brandy

ethanol (ethyl alcohol) ■

ethyl acetate ■

glycerol mono-acetate (monoacetin) ■

glycerol di-acetate (diacetin) ■

glycerol tri-acetate (tricetin) ■ solvents used to dilute and carry food colours and flavourings

glycine ■ sequestrant, buffer, nutrient

hydrogen ■

nitrogen ■ packaging gases

nitrous oxide ■ propellant used in aerosol packs of whipped cream

octadecylammonium acetate ■ anti-caking agent in yeast foods used in bread

oxygen ■ packaging gas

oxystearin ■ sequestrant, fat crystallisation inhibitor; salad cream

polydextrose ■ bulking agent; reduce and low calorie foods

propan-1, 2-diol (propylene glycol) ■

propan-2-ol (isopropyl alcohol) ■ solvents used to dilute colours and flavourings

sodium heptonate ■ sequestrant; edible oils

spermaceti ■

sperm oil ■ release agents

tannic acid ■ flavouring, clarifying agents; beer, wine and cider

122

ELIMINATION DIET — NOTES

Day 1

Time   *Food/drink*   *Reaction*

Day 2

Time   *Food/drink*   *Reaction*

Day 3

Time   *Food/drink*   *Reaction*

Day 4

Time	Food/drink	Reaction

Day 5

Time	Food/drink	Reaction

Day 6

Time	Food/drink	Reaction

Day 7

Time	Food/drink	Reaction

Day 8

Time	Food/drink	Reaction

Day 9

Time	Food/drink	Reaction

Day 10

Time	Food/drink	Reaction

Day 11

Time	Food/drink	Reaction

Day 12

Time	Food/drink	Reaction

Here is what Stan packed.

Stan packed his trumpet.

He packed his trumpet and his drum.

He packed his trumpet, his drum,
and a bandage for his thumb.

He packed his stamps.

He packed his stamps and his blocks.

He stuffed things into a box.

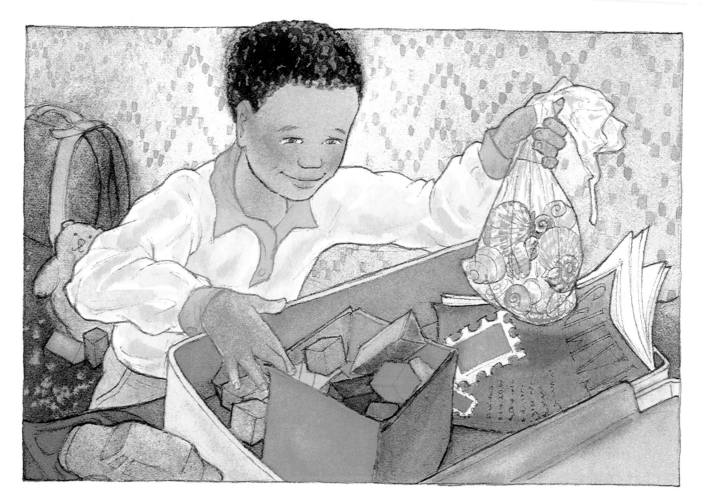

He packed his shells.

He packed his shells and his ship.

Now Stan was ready for his trip.

Should we stop him before he goes?

Stan, go check.
You need your clothes!

16